YOU WIN DEFINITELY SUCCESS IS IN YOUR HAND

SATISH KUMAR

This Book is dedicated to My mother, wife, and lovely son.

Who motivates me to do writing and is ready to listen to me every time

Contents

CHAPTER ONE

Introduction

This book contains knowledge of our leaders who got success on their life, and did a lot for our society. They changed the world and brings happiness and remove the negativity from our motherland earth.

This book will help us and provide guidance to how to achieve our aim in this world and how to make happy to our society.

This book contains the basic and fundamental things which a man should do in his life to get success, I tried to write all the things which a man should do in his life for the happiness of his own mind and for our society.

When you read this book then you come to know it is not thought to us in our childhood. This book having man basic knowledge of success and happiness.

Life is so simple whatever we want to get we can easily achieve it. We have to do only two things for that is "we have to wish and we have to work for that" then definitely we will get it.

Request you if you read this book then you should share the knowledge of this book with another person so we can make a good society and happy earth.

CHAPTER TWO

SUCCESS CAN'T BUY WE HAVE TO ACHIEVE IT

The success can't be bought but we can achieve it. for achieving we have to pay price for this, success wants hard work, it's wanted patience, it wants to sacrifice, it will give you first sorrow, insult, and a lot of pain which you have to wear then only success it will come to you and hold your hand but still it's not permanent it's only rented for you, if you want to hold its hand permanently then you should have some characteristic, you have some great habit with the help of that only you can be able to were it, I am here to give the secret of that hidden knowledge which you should know and you are deserving it. Because you have born to get success, you have born to achieved your life purpose.

We all came on earth to complete some tasks but due to unawareness, we have forgotten our real-life purpose. The real purpose of our life is to be happy and make others happy but it's not easy. Our society has made some rules and regulations that is continuously trying to take our happiness and success and are ready to give us pain and sorrow. If a person is strong physically and mentally and has wealth and power then only, he can stand as well he can help others.

This book is for those who really want to be strong physically as well as mentally, and wants wealth and power, want success and happiness.

CHAPTER THREE

GET KNOWLEDGE AND LEARN SKILLS

In our schooling, we have learned our academic materials and learned about real-life knowledge. We have to make some great habits to hold success or be successful people. We will discuss one by one those habits which were followed by our leaders. Keeping your knowledge updated and skills improving is important to further your career growth and ensure that your level of expertise is up to date. Whether it is becoming familiar with new technology or developing soft emotional intelligence skills, professional development should be a priority. It's also a great way for you to stand out from the crowd in today's competitive business world. Your knowledge and skills can be the difference between landing the clients you want and struggling to grow your business.

Having knowledge and skills above and beyond the basics of your field can give you a professional advantage.

I will tell some stories here that can help us to know the power of knowledge

Seeta as an intelligent and hardworking girl who loved to read books and always excelled in her academic tests. One day during a class lecture, Seeta's teacher asked the students, "Do you have any power?"

To this one of the students who always got first position in the school's racing competition, raised his hand and said, "Yes ma'am my power is in my legs, I can run very fast!"

"Ok. Anyone else?" the teacher looked around waiting for some other answers. Seeta then raised her hand and said, "Ma'am I have the power of knowledge. Whatever I have learnt from reading books and listening to classroom lectures, all this has contributed towards increasing my knowledge and giving me more wisdom." As Seeta finished, everyone in the classroom burst into laughter and made fun of her.

"Silent everybody!" the teacher ordered and said to Seeta, "Yes my child you are right, and all those who are laughing at you will soon get to know that knowledge is indeed a power!" The teacher's words of appreciation made seeta feel good but she could not forget the way her classmates were making fun of her.

The next day when Seeta went to school, she saw a note on the notice board. 'Who is the most intelligent student of our school?' the headline read. The notice was about the annual quiz competition. Seeta beamed with joy as she had found the way to prove to her classmates that she really does have a power — the power of knowledge!

Seeta didn't wait for a second and went to the organising committee of the quiz competition and got her name registered for participation.

The competition was to be held after a month so Seeta engrossed herself in reading books of general knowledge. She studied day and night and was very confident on the day of the quiz.

The competition began and Maria responded to all questions correctly. She won the quiz contest with 100 percent marks and got the title of 'The most intelligent student of the school'. Along with this title, she also got a trophy and two years' 100 per cent fee waiver.

The classmates of Seeta were astonished at her success and were looking at her with embarrassment on their faces.

Seeta went towards them and said, "My dear friends, physical strength is not the only power — real power lies in knowledge which does not weakened even with the passage of time." Saying this Seeta smiled and left for home to share her happiness with her family members.

I will say one more story which help us to show the power of knowledge.

An interesting incident from the Mahabharat here. Just before the great war started, both Arjun and Duryodhan, approached Krishna for assistance. Krishna was sleeping when Duryodhan entered, and he considered it below his dignity to sit at the feet of a cowherd. So he sat near Krishna's head, in a short while Arjun too entered, and he sat at Krishna's feet. When Krishna got up he saw Arjun, and greeted him, and then later greeted Duryodhan. Krishna asked Arjun what he needed for assistance, an upset Duryodhan said he came first, and so he should get the first right to ask. To which Krishna replied smartly "You came first, but it was Arjun whom I saw first, so he has the right". And then Krishna put forth his offer

"On one hand is my mighty Narayani Sena, and on the other hand is me. But I shall not take up any weapon nor take part in combat".

Given the first chance, Arjun simply asked Krishna to be his charioteer, Duryodhan on the other hand, could scarcely believe his luck. What fool would turn down an offer of the mighty Narayani Sena, he believed Arjun made a foolish decision. And walked away triumphantly, believing that the war was as good as won.

In reality Arjun knew what he was asking for, Duryodhan had the mighty Narayani Sena, but he had one man who represented that entire Army. The Kaurava army was much larger than the Pandavas, and they had some of the most formidable warriors on their side- Bhishma, Drona, Duryodhan, Karna, Kripa. Men who on their day, could rout any armyu single handed. But the Pandavas had Krishna, who knew the Kaurava forces in and out. Krishna knew the vulnerability of each and every Kaurava warrior, and he used that. Be it Bhishma, Drona or Karna, all were bought down thanks to Krishna's astute knowledge of their vulnerability.

Yes knowledge is power, but of course end of the day, you need to know how to use that knowledge. History is replete with instances of mighty armies being defeated by much smaller ones, just because the latter had better knowledge of tactics. The mighty US Army, was forced to retreat by a bunch of rag tag, ill equipped Vietnamese rebels. While the US Army was more powerful in terms of weaponry, the Vietnamese had a better knowledge of the jungle terrain and used it to their advantage. Closer home, another mighty army, that of the Mughals had to taste a humiliating defeat at the hands of the Ahoms, who were much smaller than them. Again the Ahoms, very cleverly made use of their knowledge of the river filled terrain, and exploited the weakness of the Mughal Army, in that aspect. It was the same with Shivaji, who knew that the Mughals could not face a guerilla assault and led the Marathas to many victories using the hit and run tactics.

Knowledge is power, the Pandavas had Krishna on their side, whose knowledge was so vast encompassing. All the might of the Kaurava army and their power were no match to Krishna's astute knowledge and the way he guided the Pandavas. This was the reason, why most rulers turned to priests and scholars for advice on administration, warfare, statecraft. Behind every great king and ruler, there was some one equally wise, guiding him. Chanakya made Chandragupta a king, Shivaji was molded by the wise advice of Dadaji Kondke and his mother Jijabai, and the wise minister Timmarasu, was the power behind Sri Krishnadeva Raya's glorious reign.

Knowledge is that which enables you to make the right decision. Bhima was able to kill both Jarasandh and Duryodhan, because of the advice Krishna gave to him at the right time. Knowledge ensures you work with a purpose and clarity, towards your ultimate destination. Knowledge lets you know what to do to reach your destination.

Power is essentially fickle minded, it is always not by your side. Sometimes you have it, sometimes you don't. But knowledge is the faithful partner that never leaves you, it shall always be by your side.

Here are ways to keep your job skills and knowledge up-to-date.

1. Take Professional Development Courses

Professional development courses can help you expand your professional skill set, learn something new, or even earn academic credit to put towards a degree. Online courses are particularly convenient because they are affordable and flexible. Just be careful to do your homework—evaluate instructor bios, read reviews, and check the syllabus carefully before putting down your credit card. You can also find professional development courses through vendor-taught classes, traditional universities, and training institutions.

Nowadays we used to see Engineers are doing work in banking sectors and others non-technical fields as we know that if they can lerant there professnal skill well then they can get job in there fields; its also we happened due to lack of opportunity in the system but this all excuse is only for looser not for man who is successful.

When we think of the term professional development, we automatically associate it with business managers and other leaders. However, professional development is an ongoing form of learning that will help you at any stage of your career.

Whether you're just starting out in your career or looking to take the next step up the ladder, a professional development course can help boost your skill set. It can teach you some of the fundamental skills needed in your professional life or build upon those you already have.

Different industries may update at different rates - with digital skills requiring frequent updates but the central requirements of a management role may not change as quickly. Regardless of your career focus, you will need to update your skills and knowledge throughout your career.

Along with the benefits of the course itself, you'll find many positives that come with taking a professional development course online.

Because of the flexible nature of online study, you can manage your schedule to fit around the rest of your life. So, you don't have to go to early morning classes or take time away from your family in order to update or upskill.

2. Use Online Resources

The Internet is a limitless source of free information and educational resources. Attend educational webinars, follow the blogs or social media accounts of industry experts, or bookmark and regularly check industry news sites and online forums to stay current on the latest trends. If you haven't already, sign up for news alerts for your inbox (Google Alerts works well) or set up an RSS feed like Feedly.com to easily put all of your industry news in one place.

Until very recently, people had to put a lot of effort into finding the information they needed. Students had few other options than to spend countless hours at school libraries, flipping through thousands of pages just to find what they were looking for. The introduction of the Internet, however, was a big game-changer and very soon a fantastic number of online resources became available. Still, does that mean that student research and use of resources also improved dramatically?

The best answer is that the situation is now much better, but it is far from perfect. The fact that the right information is currently available almost instantly and to any person who wishes to find it, regardless of their location, does not necessarily mean that the one who is looking for it will know where to look. It is difficult for some people to see the forest from the trees and they often get lost in the myriad of available resources. So, what can be done to make the use of online resources more effective?

BEST WAYS OF USING ONLINE RESOURCES MORE EFFECTIVELY DEVELOP INFORMATION LITERACY

If you are to use online resources effectively, you need to improve your skills in evaluating your information needs, searching for possible sources and assessing their credibility. This rarely happens overnight, but you have to be persistent and apply common sense.

You should also be able to recognize if the information you have found is outdated and you need to learn to integrate data from different sources into your assignment. Failure to do so means you'll waste your time and produce an irrelevant and useless result.

RECOGNISE RELIABLE SOURCES

It is hard to underestimate the importance of finding credible and reliable online sources. The fact that some text or information was published more recently than another one could be an indicator of the information's validity, but it does not have to be the case.

Usually, people are more interested in the source itself and are more likely to trust reputable institutions and individuals, or they rely on recommendations from their friends and colleagues. For example, there are student resources and notes platforms like Thinkswap, where study notes and guides can be downloaded and shared with other students. Here, previous students share their experiences with current and future students.

3. CHECK WHEN POSSIBLE

If you think you have found what you were looking for, make sure you crosscheck it with some other reliable resource. This is usually not very difficult, but it can be quite revealing. For instance, if no other source quotes the same information, you need to take it with a pinch of salt and keep looking.

Sometimes the credibility of the source is enough, and you can find what you need quite easily and quickly. Let's say you need to find some good university guide in Australia. A simple search will give you many resources with more or less similar lists, but the amount of information might vary.

4. RELY ON TRUSTED RECOMMENDATIONS

If someone you trust, such as your teacher, professor or expert in the particular field, recommends some resources, you should use the opportunity to avoid wasting time looking for the right information.

You can also use their suggestions to further your research using similar sources, which are recommended by the sources you were introduced to.

5. SHARING EXPERIENCE

It's always a good idea to share your experiences with various online resources with your friends and colleagues since that also cuts down the time you would spend searching. Not only does that result in increased efficiency, but you also get to see how knowledge is put into practice.

Being able to get or provide help to someone has numerous benefits, and the momentum you gain in doing so could be something that will also keep you motivated for much longer, which should result in better performance.

Although it may sometimes seem that looking for reliable online sources is overwhelming and would require a lot of time, it does not have to be like that. Those who are focused and skilled usually make the most of the availability of so many resources, and there is no reason why you should not be one of them.

Learn new technology

Technology is rapidly developing, and staying up to date on the latest advancements is key to maintaining your competitive edge. Think first about staying up to date on the technologies that directly impact your work and that your clients use. Subscribing to updates by technology creators can help you stay up to date on the latest improvements and enhancements. Also consider new technologies you might like to learn for your business such as more efficient time and expense tracking software. Search and follow experts on the technologies you can learn new features as they learn.

Can you imagine yourself becoming an accomplished Cricketer by watching tutorial videos and live matches but without stepping down on the ground or doing sufficient practice...?? Obviously not!!

The same is the case when you look forward to learning any new technology or skill. You need to follow the principle of Learn By Doing as without doing the practical implementation of all your theoretical learnings & knowledge, you can't expect to excel in the particular technology. You're required to get your hands dirty with the technology and with the respective tools to get command over it. For example, if you're learning a Programming Language or any other trending technology like Artificial Intelligence, Machine Learning, Cloud Computing, etc. – you're recommended to build several minor and major projects to get practical exposure. It will not only strengthen your fundamentals but the process will let you know about various other concepts and underlying mechanisms as well that you might not learn theoretically.

there is an approach that most of us often forget to follow but it plays a crucial role in mastering any technology. You're recommended to share your knowledge and teach others as much as you can. When you share your learning with others, it hones your skills in a greater way. This is because when you try to explain a topic to others, you first need to have an in-depth understanding and clear picture of the same in your mind that subsequently makes you proficient with that particular topic.

And here sharing your learning and teaching others doesn't only imply that you need to follow a conventional pathway and look out for the individuals to teach them but what you simply can do is write a blog or develop an online course for the particular technology to make it easier for you. Also, you can contribute to various online study groups, meetups, etc.

as per your convenience.

Whether you use online courses, training programs, YouTube videos, or any other resources – learning a new technology is always exciting and worthwhile as long as you follow the right approaches, maintain consistency, and don't give up in the mid-way. As they said that everyone in the world has the same number of hours in a day and the one who used it in the most efficient manner gets success. Hence, do follow the above-mentioned tips and utilize your time & resources efficiently to master any technology or skill out there!!

CHAPTER FOUR

Get Up Early

If you're a night owl—or an exhausted parent—waking up early and actually getting out of bed can seem insanely difficult.

The alarm goes off, but we hit snooze and then worry sleep for the next 15 minutes (or hour) until we finally manage to pull ourselves from our soft, cozy beds.

But it doesn't have to be that way. you can wake up early and start your day with energy and excitement.

Someone says well :_

MORNING IS AN IMPORTANT TIME OF DAY, BECAUSE HOW YOU SPEND YOUR MORNING CAN OFTEN TELL YOU WHAT KIND

always leaders use to say that get up early and get early. If you want to be successful in life. I am 100% a believer that our mornings determine our days. Frazzled and stressful mornings means chaotic days. Peaceful and productive mornings means calm and happy days. Because our morning lay the foundation for the rest of our day. If we start calm and centred, we're able to handle the curveballs that get thrown our way with much greater finesse. And when you have kids, the best days are when you wake up before your kids and have intentional personal time before the kids are up. You'll handle spills, tantrums, bathroom accidents with more patience and grace.

WAKE UP EARLY AND TACKLE THE DAY BEFORE IT TACKLES YOU

Never more true than for parents. Because if you wake up to a child demanding breakfast, it can feel like you're being beaten before you've even started your day. Starting te day early means you start the day on your terms, which is extremely empowering.

IF YOU WANT TO BE THE BEST, YOU CAN'T TAKE THE PATH OF LEAST RESISTANCE. EVERY MORNING, YOU WAKE UP, AND YOUR MIND TELLS YOU IT'S TOO EARLY, AND YOUR BODY TELLS YOU

YOU'RE A LITTLE TOO SORE, BUT YOU'VE GOT TO LOOK DEEP WITHIN YOURSELF AND KNOW WHAT YOU WANT AND WHAT YOU'RE STRIVING FOR

it's still hard to get out bed sometimes. But the most effective way for me to win that battle comes down to deciding what I really want.

Before you even set your alarm at night, you should ask yourself "Why do I want to get up earlier?" and really think about how it could change your life. And then when the alarm blares, you can envision the life you want–the life possible with early mornings–and find the power to get out of bed.

10 highly successful people who wake up before 6 a.m.

Here are 10 successful people who wake with (or before) the su

1. Bill McNabb, Chairman of the Vanguard Group, wakes up around 5 and gets to his desk by 6:15 a.m.

Bill McNabb, chairman and former CEO of the Vanguard Group, has a strict early-morning routine that he has not changed in decades.

"My routine has varied about 30 minutes over 30 years," he says. "When I became Vanguard's CEO in 2008 (a position I held until early 2018), I started coming in a little earlier so I could have some additional preparation time in the morning. Other than that, not much has changed since I joined the company in 1986."

His routine includes waking up between 5 and 5:15 a.m., grabbing a cup of coffee on the way to work and settling in at his desk between 5:45 and 6:15. Getting into the office early, he says, gives him crucial time for creative productivity.

"The quiet time between 6 and 7:30 a.m. is when some of my best work gets done," says McNabb. "It's my time to read, think and prepare for the day ahead. I try really hard to preserve that time."

2. Bob Ferguson, Attorney General of Washington State, wakes at 5 a.m. to make breakfast for his family

"I'm a big believer that how your day starts is really important," says Bob Ferguson, Attorney General of the state of Washington.

He wakes between 5 and 6:30 a.m. in order to carve out time for himself and his family.

"First, I have a little personal time — breakfast, coffee, the morning news," he lists. Then he wakes his children and wife up and begins to make breakfast for the family to enjoy together.

Waking up early, he explains, is the only way for him to make sure that he has time for what matters most.

"It's easy for meetings to go late at work, or for other events to come up, and I'm not always guaranteed much time with them later in the day, so I liked to lock in that morning time," says Ferguson.

3. Brad Feld, Venture Capitalist at the Foundry Group, rises anywhere between 5:30 and 9 a.m. to 'watch the day open up'

Venture capitalist Brad Feld occasionally wakes up before 6 a.m., but also warns against wearing yourself too thin.

"Five years ago, I woke up at 5 every morning during the week, regardless of what time zone I was in," he says. "Then I had a major depressive episode and decided to stop waking up with an alarm clock. I now get up whenever I wake up, which is anywhere between 5:30 and 9 a.m."

Once he wakes up, Feld weighs himself, brushes his teeth and makes a cup of coffee. He then spends four minutes sitting with his wife and their dogs. "We just sit with our coffee, talk a little and watch the day open up and the birds sing."

4. Caroline Burckle, U.S. Olympic bronze medalist, rises at 5:30 to work out — without an alarm

Like many of the other successful early-risers, Olympic swimmer Caroline Burckle wakes up early in order to work out. She wakes up around 5:30 a.m. and eats an energy bar before beginning a running interval, weight-training or swimming workout.

"I've had this routine my entire life," she says. "Swimming bred me to wake up in the wee hours of the morning from a young age. I try to have two days a week to 'sleep in' to 6:30 or 7 a.m."

What's more, Burckle says her body will naturally wake up at this early time. "Typically, my internal clock wakes me up about four minutes before my alarm," she says.

5. General Stanley McChrystal, retired U.S. Army four-star general, wakes at 4 a.m. and doesn't eat until dinner

General Stanley McChrystal's morning routine is regimented — to say the least. He wakes up around 4 a.m., shaves, exercises for an hour and a half, takes a four or five-minute shower and then goes to the office.

"When I was deployed in Iraq and Afghanistan, my morning routine was pretty much the same, except I would often break it into two parts," he says.

Even though he spends over 90 minutes working out each morning, the General skips breakfast— and lunch. "I typically don't eat anything until dinner," he says. "It just makes me feel better, my body has gotten used to it, and so if I eat before dinner I get kind of sluggish

6.Mellody Hobson, President of Ariel Investments, rises at 4 a.m. to exercise and take a bath

Mellody Hobson, who serves as the President of Ariel Investments, has been waking up before 6 a.m. for more than two decades.

She wakes up between 4 and 5 a.m. and checks her phone for urgent emails and news alerts before exercising, which consists of running, lifting weights, swimming and cycling. She drinks two liters of water while exercising. When her work out is over, she has two hard-boiled eggs with coffee or tea followed by a bath.

"My bath time is essential personal time," she explains. "I take a bath every morning, and use the time to decompress and relax. When I'm running outside on cold days in Chicago, I run faster on the return leg, thinking about my bath."

7. Melody McCloskey, founder and CEO of Style Seat, trained herself to get up at 5:45 a.m.

For Melody McCloskey, founder and CEO of Style Seat, rising with the sun is crucial to her productivity and well-being.

"I've been getting up early for a few years," she says. "For a long period of my life I stayed up very late, but I've since found my early morning routine to be the best way for me to sustain a high output and to feel balanced and happy throughout the day."

McCloskey wakes up at 5:45 a.m. and does an hour of organizing. She exercises every day at 7 a.m., either with a personal trainer or in a exercise class like hot yoga, Pilates or TRX.

"Of course, it wasn't easy at first," admits the CEO. "It was torture getting up that early; I was never naturally a morning person. But now it's become routine, and I wake up pretty early on weekends too."

8. Peter Balyta, President of Education Technology at Texas Instruments, wakes at 5:20 a.m. and does math while exercising

Growing up in Canada, Peter Balyta would wake up early every morning for hockey practice. "I'm wired to be disciplined, especially when it comes to fitness," he says.

Today, Balyta serves as the President of Education Technology for Texas Instruments. He says this discipline is a crucial part of his morning routine. Every day he wakes up at 5:20 a.m., eats a banana, drinks a glass of water, scans his email and then hits the gym.

"We start with a warm-up of light stretching, followed by a high-intensity workout of the day, involving constantly changing movements," he says.

While he is exercising he does mental math to wake up both his mind as well as his body. "Not to geek out too much, but I use simple math to determine transition times and physics to determine how to leverage my body around a barbell," he says.

9.Narendra Modi Indian Prime Minister

Narendra Modi is known to be a disciplined man. He starts his day with Surya Namaskar, Pranayam and Yoga. He sits for breakfast at 8. Breakfast for him is a typical Gujarati one.

He makes phone calls to friends and family during breakfast and heads to his office at 9:30 AM sharp.

10 Mark Zuckerberg

If you have the same kind of parents who annoy you to wake up early, here's how to tackle them. The life of Facebook's founder is as simple as his lifestyle. Mark Zuckerberg's day begins at 8 in the morning. The 31-year-old, who is seen wearing a grey tee all the time, probably heads towards his wardrobe to pick the t-shirt for the day.

However, Zuckerberg has said that many a times, he would talk to the programmers till 6 in the morning and not sleep all through the day.

you have to make these great habits which can help you to achieve your aim. I am sharing some tips and knowledge which can help you to were this habit in your daily routine.

Set an earlier bedtime

"Sleep early and wake up early" is easier said than done. But to follow that principle practically is a challenge, mostly during weekends. Watching late-night movies, going to parties, putting off important tasks till late evening delays bedtime and makes it difficult to wake up at the same time the following day.

Ideally, adults need 7-8 hours of sleep every night and on weekends the tendency to make up for staying up late is to sleep in. This practice possibly disrupts the schedule on Sundays and you feel the Monday morning blues. After experimenting with different techniques, I prefer winding up my weekend activities before bedtime. Also, strive to wake up at the same time on weekends as well and instead take a nap at noon, if need be, just to conform to the weekday routine. Training your body to fall asleep earlier may help you rise earlier each morning. Most adults should aim to get between seven and nine hours of sleep each night – anything less than that can cause you to struggle with waking up early.

Eat an early dinner. Your body needs time to absorb the food we eat. The National Sleep Foundation states that eating late dinners disturbs the sleep cycle and makes it difficult to get restful sleep. I didn't realize certain foods and dinnertime had a correlation to sleep quality. My nasal allergies became inflamed due to fried snacks late in the evening, eating rice for dinner and dairy close to bedtime. Switching to healthier options, like whole grains, whole wheat bread, less sugary fruits such as berries and pears, along with disciplining myself to eating at least three hours before bedtime, has significantly alleviated my problem with waking up early.

Unplug before bed

"Unplugging" from smartphones and laptops about 30 minutes before bed can contribute to a better night of sleep. According to Science the blue light emitted from screens can alter your body's natural melatonin levels, making it more difficult to fall asleep. An earlier bedtime with zero interference from tech can leave you feeling happier and more energized the next day.

Avoid sugary energy drinks and coffee

Energy drinks and coffee may give you the extra boost you need to study, but ingesting large amounts of sugar or caffeine before bed can make it more challenging to fall asleep and stay asleep. Limiting consumption of sugary sodas, energy drinks and coffee has been proven to produce healthier sleeping habits. Try switching to water or tea before bed to keep yourself hydrated.

Quality of sleep is as essential as quantity of sleep. According to the National Sleep Foundation, caffeine's stimulant effects increase alertness and reduces sleep quality, which could preclude you from waking up early or feeling fresh. Sometimes it is necessary to stay up to meet important work deadlines. At such times I sip on some warm water and wash my face with hot water frequently to stay alert.

Have an important reason to wake up.

We should have great reason to wake in morning. It may be some tasks or our responsibility for our family. It may Even tasks, like remembering to take an important office document, getting gas on the way to work, and giving good wishes to your spouse on her birthday, can get you enthused to wake up early.

Place your alarm clock across the room

To avoid snoozing your alarm, place your phone or alarm clock across the room from where your bed is. This way, when your alarm goes off, you'll be forced to get out of bed to silence it. Without the temptation of snoozing your alarm, you'll be up and at 'em right on time.

Training your body to wake up early will take time, so don't expect to be able to wake up at 5 a.m. every day just yet. Try implementing small changes into your routine to make early wakeups feasible, such as setting an earlier bedtime, moving the location of your alarm clock or ditching snacks and sugary drinks before bed. With these small changes, your body will eventually get in the habit of getting up early.

When you start to get up early you will get below Benefits

Enhanced Organizing Skills

Your early morning hours tend to be the most productive time of day because you get uninterrupted time to yourself. You can accomplish any task faster when you don't face distractions.

You can use this peaceful and quiet time to plan your day ahead, allocating a certain time frame for each of your tasks. Mentally working out your day before you start it enhances your organizing skills, promoting productivity.

Eat Healthy Foods

Waking up early gives you time to make a healthy breakfast. It doesn't have to be anything elaborate; smoothies, salads, and fruit bowls only require a few minutes to prepare. Early risers have this time to prepare a simple and healthy breakfast for themselves and their family. If you wake up late, chances are you'll be late for everything else, creating a domino effect. When you're running late, you'll oftentimes pick up an easy-to-eat breakfast like a doughnut or muffin, or skip breakfast altogether.

Breakfast is an important meal, giving you the energy to start the day. Skipping this meal makes your body crave energy and you end up eating something high in sugar or fat to instantly satiate yourself.

Exercise Regularly

Exercising in the morning is considered best because it gives you an adrenaline boost. Adrenaline enhances alertness, helping you overcome the sleepy feeling. Moreover, if you're in a morning exercise schedule there are fewer chances of missing it due to some other important task eating into its time. For example, if you exercise in the evening there are higher chances of missing it due to extra hours at work, a get-together with friends, or sheer exhaustion.

Beat Peak Traffic Commute

If you wake up early, you can leave your home early, beating peak traffic hours. You don't waste time being stuck in traffic while commuting to work or dropping the kids off. You'll also be on time for all your other appointments throughout the day.

Stay Stress-free

Waking up early gives you the leisure to plan your day ahead. You aren't rushing through your day in a haze with a cluttered mind. Planning ahead eliminates the stress that comes with rushing to get things done. Moreover, when you wake up early, you have more time for some stress-busting leisure activities, helping you start your day with a calm and composed mind. You are better equipped to prioritize and solve problems, the key to remaining stress-free throughout the day.

Enjoy Quality Sleep

Early risers tend to fall asleep faster. You don't have to count sheep to sleep. When you wake up early, your body feels tired early, leading to quality sleep as soon as you go to bed. You get accustomed to the natural circadian rhythm, making you early to bed and early to rise.

Longer waking hours lead to sufficient accumulation of adenosine. Adenosine is a neurotransmitter that causes sleepiness by inhibiting neuron activity. Waking up earlier leads to faster accumulation of adenosine, making you feel sleepy in the evening hours. Going to bed early improves your chances of completing all four stages of sleep through the four to six sleep cycles, making you feel well-rested and rejuvenated the next morning.

More Energy

Early birds have better sleep quality than night owls because they have higher chances of completing all stages of the required sleep cycles. They wake up with more energy than night owls, who usually don't get enough time to complete all sleep stages.

Completing sleep stages and cycles improves both physical and mental well-being. Growth hormones, causing tissue repair and regeneration, are released during the deeper stages of sleep.

Feel Happier

When you wake up early, you reap the benefits of many good habits, leading to an energetic, well-rested, stress-free, punctual, and healthy you. You get a sense of order in life, making you feel happier. In fact, according to a 2012 National Library of Medicine study, healthy adults who woke up early had a more positive state of mind than night owls.

Better Grades

Getting up early may also improve your chances of scoring higher than others in academics. In a recent study, students who woke up early in the morning got better results than those who stayed up late. On average, the early birds got a full point higher in their GPA (grade point average) than the night owls.

Better Mood and Mental Health

Individuals who wake up early have more positive thoughts compared to night owls. They're found to be more optimistic, agreeable, conscientious, and satisfied with life. Female early risers are also much less likely to develop mental illnesses, such as depression or anxiety.

People who wake up early typically go to bed earlier, as well. When you sleep the recommended 7 to 9 hours, your body and mind have enough time to restore themselves, resulting in a healthier body and mind.

CHAPTER FIVE

MAKE HABIT OF READING AND WRITING

It does not matter in which profession you belong you should make a habit to morning writing and reading. This habit will help you to get knowledge and organize your ideas and thoughts. Good reader's speed should be 600 to 700 words per minute. If you have that much speed you are a genius if you don't have then you have to improve it.

Reading is a very good habit that one needs to develop in life. Good books can inform you, enlighten you and lead you in the right direction. There is no better companion than a good book. Reading is important because it is good for your overall well-being. Once you start reading, you experience a whole new world. When you start loving the habit of reading you eventually get addicted to it. Reading develops language skills and vocabulary. Reading books is also a way to relax and reduce stress. It is important to read a good book at least for a few minutes each day to stretch the brain muscles for healthy functioning.

Books really are your best friends as you can rely on them when you are bored, upset, depressed, lonely or annoyed. They will accompany you anytime you want them and enhance your mood. They share with you information and knowledge any time you need. Good books always guide you to the correct path in life. Following are the benefits of reading –

Self-Improvement: Reading helps you develop positive thinking. Reading is important because it develops your mind and gives you excessive knowledge and lessons of life. It helps you understand the world around you better. It keeps your mind active and enhances your creative ability. There is number of self-help books that can change a person life, book gives us knowledge to be a perfect man and live life as he dreams. When you read an inspiring book every day, you flood your brain with positive words and uplifting concepts. Making the time for this raises your vibration and keeps you in optimal conditions more often than not.

A lot of personal development books come with exercises and prompts that get you thinking about the choices you make and why you make them. An honest evaluation of your life as it is freeing you to make the changes you need to make while still feeling good about yourself.

When you're aware of the thinking behind your actions, you can erase your negative thought tapes and replace them with words of love, possibility, power, and magic. This makes you super aware of what you choose to fill your day with, so you can do more of what's working, and less of what's not.

Reading an inspiring book, a day isn't to improve your life — it's to enhance your life. The whole point of personal development is to expand more of what you've got, not improve what you think is lacking. When you approach each book as a treasure map to discover hidden knowledge, you adopt a playful, curious attitude that lets you explore each book from a grounded, expansive place.

You start to believe you can be more, do more and experience more. A daily diet of inspiring words spurs you to explore what you're capable of, and where your limitations lie so you can smash through them. This is how you get stronger and better — you dare yourself to go where you haven't gone before, so you can experience what you haven't had before. When we believe we can be more, we're pulled to do and feel more.

Communication Skills: Reading improves your vocabulary and develops your communication skills. It helps you learn how to use your language creatively. Not only does it improve your communication but it also makes you a better writer. Good communication is important in every aspect of life. In a world where information is the new currency, reading is one of the best sources of continuous learning, knowledge gathering and idea sharing. Books and articles give us the ability to roam throughout the world, travel back in time and look to the future, affording us with a deeper view of ideas, concepts, practices, emotions and events. Reading can open your mind to new choices that you may not have known about or considered before. This is all information which we can then share with others. The more we read, the more our brains are able to link cause and effect. The ability to communicate cause and effect is a central component of any argument, sales pitch, negotiation or story. As such, a well-written article or book will be structured in a way that helps us to think in sequence rather than jumping from point to point.

The first rule of effective communication is to know your audience. Reading about other people can help you understand them better. The same neurological regions of the brain are stimulated when you read about something as when you experience it. Unlike watching the television or listening to the radio, reading gives the brain more time to stop, think, process and imagine the narrative form in front of us. Therefore, reading can help put you in someone else's shoes, to get inside their heads and experience the things they have. The more you understand someone, the more you can tailor your communications to what they need.

Increases Knowledge: Books enable you to have a glimpse into cultures, traditions, arts, history, geography, health, psychology and several other subjects and aspects of life. You get an amazing amount of knowledge and information from books. While reading, your brain must remember facts and details such as characters, plots and subplots. As your brain retains this information, you're creating new memories. That means new synapses are being created, and old ones are being strengthened. This improves your short term and long-term memory functions

Reduces Stress: Reading a good book takes you in a new world and helps you relieve your day-to-day stress. It has several positive effects on your mind, body, and soul. It stimulates your brain muscles and keeps your brain healthy and strong. In a 2009 study from the consultancy Mind lab International at the University of Sussex, testing found that reading reduced stress levels by 68 percent, making it a more effective means of relaxation than taking a walk, drinking a cup of tea, or playing video games. Reading books, particularly fiction, fully engages the mind and imagination. Any activity that possesses meditative qualities in which the brain is fully focused on a single task is proven to reduce stress and enhance relaxation. In a study conducted by the University of Sussex, individuals who had read for merely six minutes exhibited slower heart rates, less muscle tension, and reduced stress levels. Dr. David Lewis, the neuroscientist who conducted the study, reported that reading, "is more than merely a distraction but an active engaging of the imagination as the words on the printed page stimulate your creativity and cause you to enter what is essentially an altered state of consciousness." It turns out getting lost in a good book truly is the ultimate form of relaxation. The benefits of reading expand beyond reduced anxiety and stress. Studies have linked reading to good brain health in old age. Individuals who read regularly across their lifespan showed increased mental capacity as they aged. Those individuals who read less frequently throughout their life and did not continue to engage their brains in old age experienced a mental decline rate that was 48 percent faster than those who kept their brains active across their lives. One study found a positive association between cognitive based activities such as reading and a decreased chance of developing Alzheimer's disease. Just like the heart, the brain is a muscle that needs to be taken care of in order to function at its fullest capacity throughout our lifetimes.

One in five adults in the United States experience a mental illness at some point in their lives. Reading self-help books has proven to be an effective method for helping adults cope with mental illness. In the UK, doctors have embraced the approach of using bibliotherapy, or treatment through the use of books, for patients with mental health conditions. Doctors have been incorporating required reading as part of a patient's prescription. The goal is to bring the benefits of reading to as if stress reduction, improved mental health, and healthy brain function weren't enough, reading can also help individuals become more empathetic and increase their self-awareness. In particular, reading literary fiction can increase one's understanding of others and improve relationships. As readers become engrossed in a storyline, they empathize with characters and learn their motivations and behaviour patterns. This increases a person's understanding of human behaviour which is knowledge that carries over to life outside of a novel. Furthermore, when readers select novels that are set in locations with cultures other than their own, they further develop an awareness of diverse human populations and perspectives. With all of these benefits, there is no doubt that reading is truly the powerhouse of leisure activities. People who read often, become more empathetic. Reading is to the mind what exercise is to the body." Hundreds of years later, this quote could not be truer. Studies conducted over the last few decades have proven the scientific benefits of reading. Curling up with a good book is not only enjoyable, it can positively impact your mental and emotional health.

It is a proven fact that reading can help reduce stress. Many of us take this simple act for granted, because we have so much "required" reading in our daily lives-the newspaper, traffic signs, emails, and bills. But how often do we read for pleasure?

Reading can be a wonderful (and healthy) escape from the stress of everyday life. Simply by opening a book, you allow yourself to be invited into a literary world that distracts you from your daily stressors. Reading can even relax your body by lowering your heart rate and easing the tension in your muscles. It works better and faster than other relaxation methods, such as listening to music or drinking a hot cup of tea. This is because your mind is invited into a literary world that is free from the stressors that plague your daily life.

Great Pleasure: When I read a book, I read it for pleasure. I just indulge myself in reading and experience a whole new world. Once I start reading a book, I get so captivated I never want to leave it until I finish. It always gives a lot of pleasure to read a good book and cherish it for a lifetime. Reading is not just something that children should do in school, it needs to be an everyday part of our lives and something we choose to do at all ages.

Research has also shown that students who choose what and where they read tend to be more motivated, read more and show greater language and literacy development. The study by academics at the Institute of Education, part of the University of London, found that reading had the strongest effect on vocabulary development but the impact on maths and spelling was also significant.

Boosts your Imagination and Creativity: Reading takes you to the world of imagination and enhances your creativity. Reading helps you explore life from different perspectives. While you read books you are building new and creative thoughts, images and opinions in your mind. It makes you think creatively, fantasize and use your imagination. Reading is fun and engaging, but one of the most entertaining parts of reading is probably stepping into another world and immersing yourself in that book's setting.

Whether it is a new realm, fighting off dragons or trying to survive in a dystopia, it becomes obvious that reading improves imagination. Your imagination is the one that lets you get transported in the magical world between the pages of a good work of fiction. Well, now, who hasn't heard about Albert Einstein? We've all heard about him, right? But did you know that he believed that imagination is more important than knowledge? He thought that someone who has great imagination also has the ability to create and discover more than the average not so imaginative human.

Nowadays, scientists have come to the conclusion that reading can indeed help broaden your imagination by stimulating the right side of the brain. We might even go as far as to say that reading literally opens up our minds to new concepts and possibilities.

Imagination has a lot of proven benefits: it encourages creativity and innovative thinking. Without imagination playing its part, people wouldn't be able to come up with new ideas or inventions that help advance our society as a whole. And reading is a key part of enhancing imagination.

there's no denying that, for sure. Our brains need to be kept active in order to stay healthy and reading is a great exercise for the mind. The more you read, the better you concentrate and the better you will be able to imagine ideas and new concepts.

Develops your Analytical Skills: By active reading, you explore several aspects of life. It involves questioning what you read. It helps you develop your thoughts and express your opinions. New ideas and thoughts pop up in your mind by active reading. It stimulates and develops your brain and gives you a new perspective. Reading books is not only an effective way how to improve analytical skills, it's also fun! Find out what analytical skills are and how you can improve them by reading fiction

Analytical skills are defined as the ability to visualize, conceptualize, and solve both simple and complex problems using all information available. Analytical skills can include a wide array of different skills, but all of them are necessary for critical thinking and adept problem solving. We use these skills every day, from riding a bike to planning an event. Gathering information is another important part of analytical thinking and it requires more effort than you might think! This is largely because you don't know what you don't know. To discover this, you have to know where to find information to fill in the gaps. You can do this by observing phenomena in your own life or by reading a scientific article.

Regular reading has a positive impact on brain function. It stimulates the brain and allows a child to think analytically.

When a child is actively engaged in reading, they gain different perspectives, ask questions, identify patterns, and make connections. And the more they read, the more they can easily spot patterns, which helps build their critical thinking and analytical skills.

Reading requires keeping up with different characters and remembering what happened and to whom. The reader also needs to make predictions and conclusions. This keeps their brain active.

The kids of today spend a lot of time on the internet, sometimes even more than adults. This keeps their brain in constant motion and makes thinking analytically harder. The brain is like a muscle; it needs regular exercise to remain alert and agile, and reading is a great way to achieve this.

Reduces Boredom: Journeys for long hours or a long vacation from work can be pretty boring in spite of all the social sites. Books come in handy and release you from boredom.

The habit of reading is one of the best qualities that a person can possess. Books are known to be your best friend for a reason. So it is very important to develop a good reading habit. We must all read on a daily basis for at least 30 minutes to enjoy the sweet fruits of reading. It is a great pleasure to sit in a quiet place and enjoy reading. Reading a good book is the most enjoyable experience one can have.

I will now be discussed how to increase your reading speed.

Do daily reading- Reading has a number of benefits including improving your memory and vocabulary, helping you learn new things, and improving focus and concentration. A lot of people say that they want to develop a reading habit but are unable to due to a lack of time. I was one of those people myself at one point in my life. I have used a number of tricks to help me read more and develop a daily reading habit. I have outlined these below

Create a reading list I would definitely suggest you start out by creating a list of books that you would like to read. For example, you could create a list of novels you've always wanted to read but never had the chance to, or a list of books that you need to read to learn something about a topic or field of study that you are interested in. Apart from creating your own lists, you can also use lists that other people have created.

Set a goal A good idea to motivate yourself to read more is to set a goal. For example, you could set a goal to read a certain number of books this year or a certain number of pages each day and then work on reaching that goal. Some tools you can use to help you achieve your reading goals include the Bookly app and the GoodReads.com Reading Challenge.

Schedule a time for reading

To make sure that you will read every day, you need to schedule reading into your day. You could read first thing in the morning, during your commute, before going to sleep or even during lunch.

Find a good place to read

Something that will help you read more is finding a good place to read. This should preferably be somewhere quiet, without any distractions. You could read in your bed, in a comfortable chair or sofa, on a park bench, and of course — at the library.

Eliminate distractions

Make sure to eliminate any distractions that might be interfering with your reading — turn off the TV and put your smartphone on silent.

Read actively

While passive reading is better than no reading at all, I would highly suggest you try an active approach to reading. When I say "read actively", I mean think about what you are reading, highlight passages that you think are important or interesting, write comments and notes either on the book's margins or in a separate notebook. If you are reading on your smartphone or your ebook reader, take advantage of their highlighting and note features.

Keep a reading journal

I highly recommend keeping a reading journal where you can write down quotes that you like, record what books you have read, jot down any thoughts related to the book as well as any comments you have on what you have read. You can review these later to refresh your memory or to get new ideas.

Carry a book everywhere you go

Always carry some reading material with you, either in the form of a physical book, or an ebook on your smartphone or ebook reader. That way you're able to read whenever you get a chance. This allows you to spend those little breaks in your day reading instead of scrolling your Facebook or Instagram feed.

Know when to quit

Don't feel like you have to finish every book you start. If the book you're reading is boring or not what you imagined it would be, simply drop it and start reading a different one. A good rule that I like to use is the 50-page rule. I always read the first 50 pages of any book I start. If I still don't enjoy it after 50 pages, I just quit and move on to a different book.

Replace other forms of entertainment with reading

A good way to read more is to replace other forms of entertainment with reading. For example, instead of watching TV or movies, playing video games, or mindlessly browsing the Explore tab on Instagram — read a book. This will allow you to read a lot more books every year.

Read multiple books at the same time

Something I like to do is read multiple books at the same time. Anytime I get bored with a book or I would like a change of pace, I just switch to a different one. A great way to do this is to always read one fiction book and one non-fiction book at the same time.

Get a reading partner

You can also get a reading partner to help you keep yourself accountable to your reading goals. This can be a friend of yours, a significant other, or a colleague. You can start reading the same book with your reading partner and then discuss it as you read or once you both finish reading the book.

I hope these tips will help you to read more and develop a daily reading habit. Now go and read a book!

If you make a particular time for reading it will definitely will help you to improve your reading skills.

Improve speed –

Speed reading is the process of rapidly recognizing and absorbing phrases or sentences on a page all at once, rather than identifying individual words.

The amount of information that we process seems to be growing by the day, whether it's emails, reports and websites at work, or social media, books and magazines at home. Firstly, you start to read word by word then we read sentence by sentence and then we read line by line and then we read page by page. It is possible when you will do continually practicing of improving your reading skills, If you get this skill I will say you can easily achieve your reading goals. You will never feel bored when you can read fastly.

The first bad reading habit is subvocalization. "It's that little voice in your head you use from time to time when you read. From a young age, many of us are taught to read aloud, and as we progress, we then read inside our heads, Often, we might not even be aware we're doing this. Why is this a problem? Because people's average speaking speeds are 100–160 words per minute, our reading speeds consequently suffer. "If we want to read faster, we must start to see the words as opposed to hear them," One quick trick is to press the tip of your tongue to the roof of your mouth as you read. it will prevent you from unintentionally mouthing the words and also provides a distraction for your brain.

You might also try listening to classical or instrumental music while you read. This can help mute your reading-aloud inner voice and puts you in a state conducive for engagement.

The second bad reading habit is regression. No, this isn't about your fondness for young-adult novels or comic books; those are absolutely fine. Regression is when you get to the end of a page or halfway through an article and realize you haven't taken in what you read. Or you come across a particular person or term and can't remember them at all. You end up having to go back and start all over. This can happen over and over and over again. The reason for this isn't a lack of understanding, but a lapse in concentration. Even though we think we've been diligently reading, we've become distracted.

How to change it: You can start by reigniting your interest in what you're reading. "When our brain wanders, it's because we've become passive. We need to be curious,"

Get actively inquisitive — tap into your inner curious kid, the one who demands, "But what does that mean?" and "Who's that?" Other questions recommended "What am I looking for?" and "What key words and figures do I need to find?" You might also check in every few minutes and simply ask yourself, "What have I learned so far?"

Another method for tackling this problem is called gliding. Using an object like a credit card or an envelope, cover up sentences as soon as you read them; move the shield down your page (or device) as you progress.

"The great thing about gliding is it removes your safety net to re-read the sentence you've just read — meaning you've got to pay attention to the sentence you're reading because you know there's no way you can go back."

One final strategy is external — choose surroundings that will allow you to concentrate when you read. For some people, this could mean places with library-like silence. But if that doesn't work for you,

trying a coffee shop where other people are working. Many cafes, he says, "have learned to create an environment which is optimum for productivity — not too loud, where you get distracted by what's going on around you, and not too quiet, where your brain begins to wander."

The third bad reading habit is fixation. Fixations are the points on the page or screen our eyes alight on as we read; we can end up inadvertently lingering on random spots, which impedes our speed.

How to change it: using a pacer — a tool to point at sentences as you read them, which can train your eyes to keep moving. It could be your finger, a pen, even your cursor. This has two main benefits,

"One, it maintains our reading speed. Often, when we read, we don't realize how fast or slow we're reading until it's too late. Number two, it increases and encourages our eyes to read faster because we're forced to read an accelerated way."

By deploying these habits and using some other shortcuts we can read fastly.

But he wants people to know that speed reading is "a superpower which you can turn on and off." In the same way that you change your walking speed given the context — you'll stroll in a park and race-walk to reach the supermarket before it closes — you should adjust how you're reading depending on whether it's for enjoyment or for need. So, when you've settled in to consume whatever it is that you read for pleasure, take some time to savor it.

CHAPTER SIX

LEARN WRITING SKILL

Jason Fried says in his book Rework that in Basecamp, company in which he is co-founder and CEO, one of the abilities that they are interested in when hiring people is their writing ability, no matter if they are sales people, programmers, or designers. The reason is simple: Clear writing is a sign of clear thinking. Good writers know how to communicate, they make things easy to understand and they know when to leave out the unnecessary.

Does this mean that you have to attend literature and grammar classes to be more effective when carrying out your tasks? No, you already have all the necessary knowledge. You learn how to write by writing. If you get used to express this way your ideas, feelings, goals, etc., you will achieve important benefits:

1. You will communicate with clarity. Unlike talking, when you write you look for more sophisticated words and expressions to describe what you have in mind. This helps you build a structure that will allow you to express yourself better and communicate complex ideas in a much more effective way.

2. You will eliminate stress. In the same way as in GTD you empty your mind—by capturing everything that comes to it—in order to eliminate the stress that causes having many things hitting your head, writing and developing your ideas produces an amplified effect since not only you take them out of your mind but also the whole process of rationalization that otherwise would abstractly stay in there.

3. You will be more productive. Writing activates the neurons in your brain and gets it ready to overcome the rest of the tasks (you can use it as a kind of warm-up at the beginning of the day). In addition, writing down your tasks with the appropriate words prepares you to carry them out properly. Finally, it's demonstrated that setting your goals in writing increases significantly the possibilities of achieving them.

4. You will learn more. Writing in your own words the information that you receive helps you assimilating and consolidating knowledge that otherwise you would forget soon.

5. You will gain awareness of your reality. If you write down what you have in mind each day, what you expect to achieve and how you feel according to this, you won't need a psychologist to explain you who you are. You will realize yourself.

It

6. You will make better decisions. When writing you clear up your thoughts and, obviously, a clearer thinking allows you to make better choices.

7. You will be happier. It's an immediate consequence of the two previous points. There is no need to write a public blog, a sort of personal journal is perfectly valid.

8. You will live more focused. If you constantly write about your thoughts you will never get out of sight what you want to achieve, which your dreams are.

9. You will overcome tough moments faster. There is some research that suggests that those that write about what is happening overcome tough moments quicker than those who don't.

10. You will have a lot of written memories. If you write each day, you will have a historical record of your thoughts, probably something much more interesting than a simple photo album. And, who knows, maybe you end up publishing a book ;)

So write a lot and write every day.

Ways to Improve Writing skills.

From sending emails to preparing presentations, writing is often a day-to-day task in many professions spanning diverse industries. Writing skills go beyond grammar and spelling. Accuracy, clarity, persuasiveness, and several other elements play a part in ensuring your writing is conveying the right message.Writing is a technical skill that allows you to communicate effectively through the written word. Though these may vary depending on what you're writing, there are several that transcend categories. Writing skills can more specifically include:

- Grammar
- Vocabulary
- Spelling
- Sentence construction

- Structure
- Research and accuracy
- Clarity
- Persuasiveness

Each of these components can influence the quality of writing.

Writing, like any other skill, is something we can get better at with time and practice. Here are some strategies for developing your own written communication:

Make Writing a Daily Exercise

Practice really does make perfect! If you compare writing to a skill like cooking, or even playing a sport, you cannot expect to improve if you don't practice – it's like expecting to become a pro football player after one practice with your team.

Try to set yourself daily writing exercises – they need not be long-winded and time-consuming, even just committing yourself to writing a paragraph a day is enough! You can even partner up with someone else who also wants to improve their writing skills and read each other's paragraphs to see where changes need to be made.

Read, Read, and Read Some More!

We learn best by example, and gaining writing skills is no exception to this rule. When we read, we learn how other people write to convey their messages in the best way possible, and we start to adapt our writing styles to those that we resonate most with.

Incorporate daily reading into your writing exercises; maybe even make your practice paragraph a review or summary of what you read that day, taking different elements of the author's writing style to develop your own voice.

Be Succinct

Try not to use any complicated, long words in your writing. They often confuse the reader and make them disinterested in what you have to say. Keep your sentences short. Never over-use filler words like "very", "really", "just", etc.

They tend to make sentences long and unnecessarily take up your reader's cognitive space.

Develop a Clear Message

There is nothing more frustrating than a piece of writing that doesn't get straight to the point. Think about what you want to say, what message you want your reader to take away with them, and make sure that that you make this message clear from the very beginning.

It is also important to think about your audience; what do they want to hear, and how would they like it to be conveyed? Do you need to take on a formal, or a more informal tone? Would using humour help develop your message, or should you get straight to the point in a more business-like fashion?

These are important considerations that need to be taken into account before you even begin the writing process.

Sit Down and Write!

Sometimes the most difficult step in the writing process is the act of actually sitting down and getting the writing done. By this point, you should have a clear plan of what you want to say, and a general idea of how you want to say it.

It may seem daunting, but remember that the hard work is now done! All you need to do is convince yourself that you are capable (which you are), sit down in front of your n0tebook or computer, and execute your communication!

Review grammar and spelling basics.

Grammar and spelling form the foundation of good writing. Writing with proper grammar and spelling communicates your professionality and attention to detail to your reader. It also makes your writing easier to understand.

Plus, knowing when and how to use less-common punctuation, like colons, semicolons, and em-dashes, can unlock new ways to structure sentences and elevate your writing.

If you're looking to strengthen your grammar and spelling, start by consulting a writing manual. The Elements of Style by William Stunk and E.B. White has long been considered a staple for writers. You can find similar resources at your local library, bookstore, or online.

Read what you want to write.

Knowing what a finished piece of writing can look like can guide your own. If you're trying to write a humorous short story, read humorous short stories. Writing a book review? Find a few and take note of how they're structured. Pay attention to what makes them good and what you want to emulate (without plagiarizing, of course). If you're working on a school assignment, you can ask your instructor for examples of successful pieces from past students.

Make reading a part of your everyday life to improve your writing. Try reading the news in the morning or picking up a book before you head to bed. If you haven't been a big reader in the past, start with topics you're interested in, or ask friends and family for recommendations. You'll gradually begin to understand what subjects, genres, and authors you enjoy.

Proofread.

While it's tempting to submit work as soon as you're done with it, build in some time to revisit what you've written to catch errors big and small. Here are a few proofreading tips to keep in mind:

• **Set your work aside before you edit**. Try to step away from your writing for a day or more so you can come back to it with fresh, more objective eyes. Crunched for time? Even allotting 20 minutes between writing and proofreading can allow you to approach your work with renewed energy.

• **Start with easy fixes**, then progress to bigger changes. Starting with easier changes can get you in the rhythm for proofreading, allow you to read through your work once more, and clear distractions so you can focus on bigger edits. Read through your work to catch misspellings, inconsistencies, and grammar errors. Then address the larger problems with structure or awkward transitions.

• **If you could say something in fewer words**, do so. Being unnecessarily wordy can cloud your message and confuse the reader. Pare down phrases that are redundant, repetitive, or obvious.

• Read out loud. Reading out loud can help you find awkward phrases and areas where your writing doesn't flow well.

Get feedback.

Whether you're writing emails or essays, asking for feedback is a great way to see how somebody besides yourself will interpret your text. Have an idea of what you'd like your proof-reader to focus on—the structure, conclusion, the persuasiveness of an argument, or otherwise.

Approach a trusted friend, family member, co-worker, or instructor. If you're a student, your school might also have a writing resource centre you can reach out to.

You might also consider forming a writing group or joining a writing class. Find writing courses online, at your local community college, or at independent writing workshops in your city.

5. Think about structure.

Grammar and spelling keep your writing consistent and legible, but structure ensures the big ideas get across to the reader.

In many cases, forming an outline will help solidify structure. An outline can clarify what you're hoping to convey in each section, enable you to visualize the flow of your piece, and surface parts that require more research or thought.

Structure might look different depending on what you're writing. An essay typically has an introduction, body paragraphs, and a conclusion. A fiction piece might follow the six-stage plot structure: exposition, rising action, climax, falling action, resolution, and denouement. Choose what's best for your purposes.

Write.

Like many skills, one of the best ways to improve your writing is to practice. Here are a few ways you can get started:

• Start a journal or a blog.

• Join a class or writing workshop.

• Practice free writing.

• Write letters to friends or family.

• Put together an opinion piece for your local newspaper or publication you like.

Know some common fixes.

Even if a text is grammatically correct, you may be able to make it more dynamic and interesting with some polish. Here are some common ways you can sharpen your writing:

• Choose strong verbs (for example, "sprinted," "dashed," or "bolted" instead of "ran").

• Avoid passive voice.

• Vary sentence length.

• Cut unnecessary words.

• Replace cliches with original phrasing.

CHAPTER SEVEN

INCREASE MENTAL AND PHYSICAL STRENGHT

A power that will help you to recall that you know Is mental power. If a person has a great recall power, then he can remember all the knowledge which he gains and he can utilize them. He can get memorize things easily. He can get good academic records; he can be a great scientist and leaders and many more things he Can get if he has great mental power.

Physical fitness gets a lot of attention, and for good reason—good physical health can prevent conditions such as heart disease or diabetes, and help you maintain a long, independent life. But often neglected is mental fitness—having a healthy and strong mind to allow you to handle the challenges and opportunities that life puts in front of you.

A common thought is that the absence of a mental health disorder means that a person is mentally fit and emotionally well

"Mental wellness is a process, and just like physical health, it's an ongoing process to maintain mental and emotional wellness."

Unsurprisingly, trying or stressful times can be the ultimate test of mental fitness. When we are winded by a major life event, being able to recover quickly requires significant mental strength and psychological resilience. The benefits of being mentally fit means we are able to use our mental abilities to our fullest extent, allowing us to be more creative, make the most of opportunities as they present themselves, and approach stressful situations more calmly and with less anxiety.

So, what can you do to increase your mental fitness levels?

Focus on One Thing at a Time

Multitasking is worn as a badge of honor, but multitasking too much is not healthy. Practice being present. When you are taking a walk, take in your surroundings—the weather, the birds. When you are spending time with friends, really listen to what is being said. Turn off your phone and try to forget the running to-do lists in your head.

Reframe negative thoughts.

If you are having catastrophic thoughts like "This will never work," then replace them with something more realistic, like "If I work hard, I'll improve my chances of success."

It's true that everyone has bad days that lead to negative thoughts. But by searching for positive and realistic expectations, you can eliminate these damaging pessimistic thoughts and better equip yourself to manage the bad days.

Create goals.

It's fun to aim high and dream big. But setting your sights too high will likely lead to disappointment.

Rather than set out to lose 100 pounds, focus on losing five first. When you crush that goal, you'll be more motivated to lose the next five pounds.

Every goal you achieve gives you confidence in your own ability to be successful. This will also help you identify which goals are not challenging enough and which ones are unrealistically ambitious.

Give Yourself a Daily "Mindfulness Break"

Set aside one to two minutes each day to decompress, check in with your body, and assess how you're feeling," O'Neill said. "There are a number of great apps that can help you incorporate a structured mindfulness practice or you can simply develop a practice that works for you."

Just one week of brief daily mindfulness meditation practice has been found to produce significant improvements in attention, energy, and stress. Research shows these benefits are more than just subjective: participants of a study experienced actual decreases in stress-controlled cortisol and improvement in their immune system. They also displayed improved visuospatial processing, working memory, and executive functioning—important sets of mental skills that help you get things done faster.

Don't Be Afraid to Reach Out for Help

Seeking help is often the first step towards getting and staying well, but it can be hard to know how to start or where to turn to. It's common to feel unsure, and to wonder whether you should try to handle things on your own.

Remember that it's okay to say "no" sometimes.

"But to put it simply, there's never a wrong time to seek help

"Talking with someone about your thoughts and feelings can always help you to gain insight that will likely be beneficial in your life. If you find yourself experiencing periods of stress, or feeling angry, irritable, sad, or easily frustrated, it could be a good invitation to seek out professional help to deal with those feelings."

Mental fitness doesn't have to take up a lot of your time. Spending a few minutes on it every day can help you feel better and think more clearly. Remember that relaxation is just as important in a mental workout as the more energetic activities, such as memory exercises or physical exercise.

Set yourself up for success.

You don't need to subject yourself to temptations every day to stay mentally strong. Modify your environment from time to time. Make life a little easier.

Put your running sneakers next to the bed if you want to work out in the morning. Remove the junk food from your pantry if your goal is to eat healthier. Little things like this will go a long way toward keeping you from exhausting your own mental energy and setting yourself up for success.

Do at least one difficult thing each day.

Improvement doesn't come about by accident. You need to challenge yourself on purpose. Make sure to analyse your own boundaries, though, since everyone has a different idea of what is challenging.

Have the courage to pick something slightly outside these boundaries. And then take one small step every day.

Enroll in a class you don't think you qualify for. Speak up for yourself even when it is uncomfortable. Always push yourself to become a little better today than you were yesterday.

Tolerate discomfort for a greater purpose.

The feeling of discomfort can often lead people to look for unhealthy shortcuts. Binge TV-watching and over drinking are common emotional crutches. But these types of short-term solutions more often create bigger long-term problems.

The next time you experience discomfort, remind yourself of the bigger picture. Finish that workout even when you are tired. Balance your budget even when it gives you anxiety. Tolerating uncomfortable emotions can help you gain the confidence you need to crush your goals.

Balance your emotions with logic.

If you were to be 100 percent logical all the time, you might live a boring life, devoid of leisure time, pleasure, or even love. But if you base all of your decisions on emotion, you might spend all your money on fun, rather than save for retirement or investments. To make the best decisions, you need to balance your logic and emotion.

So regardless of how minor or major the decision in your life, check yourself to make sure you are balancing your emotions with logic.

Being overly anxious, angry, or excited can cause you to make an emotional decision. So write down a list of pros and cons for each decision you make. Reviewing this list will enhance the logical part of your brain and help balance out your emotions.

Fulfil your purpose.

It's hard to stay the course unless you know your overall purpose. Why is it that you want to hone your craft or to earn more money?

Write out a clear and concise mission statement about what you want to accomplish in life. When you're struggling to take the next step, remind yourself why it's important to keep going. Focus on your daily objectives, but make sure those steps you're taking will get you to a larger goal in the long run.

Look for explanations, not excuses.

Did you fall short of your goal? Then examine the reasons. Rather than make excuses for your behaviour, look for an explanation than can help you do better next time.

Take on the full responsibility for any shortcomings without placing blame. When you face and acknowledge your mistakes, you can learn from them and avoid repeating them.

Use the 10-minute rule.

Mental strength can help you be productive when you don't feel like it. But it's not a magic wand that will make you feel motivated all the time.

There is a 10-minute rule that comes in handy when you are tempted to put off something important. If you catch yourself eyeing the couch at the time you planned to go for your mile run, then tell yourself to get moving for just 10 minutes. If your mind is still fighting your body after 10 minutes, then it might be OK to give yourself permission to quit.

But more often than not, once you take that first step, you'll realize your task is not nearly as tough as you predicted. Getting started is almost always the hardest part, but your other learned skills can help keep you going.

Prove yourself wrong.

The next time you think you can't do something, prove yourself wrong. Commit to topping your sales goal for this month or beating your time in the mile run.

You are more capable than you give yourself credit for, so make it a habit to prove yourself wrong. Over time, your brain will stop underestimating your own potential.

This power we can increase by practicing and do some exercise

I will be going to discussed about tricks and exercise which helps you to get great mental power

Don't use a calculator _

you should don't use a calculator until its not needed. Start to make small bills settlements in your finger. let them to do work to your mind. If possible, don't use even pen and paper also.

CHAPTER EIGHT

Do Meditation

When we meditate, we inject far-reaching and long-lasting benefits into our lives: We lower our stress levels, we get to know our pain, we connect better, we improve our focus, and we're kinder to ourselves. Let us walk you through the basics in our new mindful guide on how to meditate

How do you learn to meditate?

how to pay attention to the breath as it goes in and out, and notice when the mind wanders from this task. This practice of returning to the breath builds the muscles of attention and mindfulness.

When we pay attention to our breath, we are learning how to return to, and remain in, the present moment—to anchor ourselves in the here and now on purpose, without judgement.

While meditation isn't a cure-all, it can certainly provide some much-needed space in your life. Sometimes, that's all we need to make better choices for ourselves, our families, and our communities. And the most important tools you can bring with you to your meditation practice are a little patience, some kindness for yourself, and a comfortable place to sit.

When we meditate, we inject far-reaching and long-lasting benefits into our lives. And bonus: you don't need any extra gear or an expensive membership.

Here are five reasons to meditate:

1. Understanding your pain
2. Lower your stress
3. Connect better
4. Improve focus
5. Reduce brain chatter

How to Meditate

Meditation is simpler (and harder) than most people think. Read these steps, make sure you're somewhere where you can relax into this process, set a timer, and give it a shot:

1) Take a seat

Find place to sit that feels calm and quiet to you.

2) Set a time limit

If you're just beginning, it can help to choose a short time, such as five or 10 minutes.

3) Notice your body

You can sit in a chair with your feet on the floor, you can sit loosely cross-legged, you can kneel—all are fine. Just make sure you are stable and, in a position, you can stay in for a while.

4) Feel your breath

Follow the sensation of your breath as it goes in and as it goes out.

5) Notice when your mind has wandered

Inevitably, your attention will leave the breath and wander to other places. When you get around to noticing that your mind has wandered—in a few seconds, a minute, five minutes—simply return your attention to the breath.

6) Be kind to your wandering mind

Don't judge yourself or obsess over the content of the thoughts you find yourself lost in. Just come back.

7) Close with kindness

When you're ready, gently lift your gaze (if your eyes are closed, open them). Take a moment and notice any sounds in the environment. Notice how your body feels right now. Notice your thoughts and emotions.

That's it! That's the practice. You focus your attention, your mind wanders, you bring it back, and you try to do it as kindly as possible (as many times as you need to.

How Much Should I Meditate?

Meditation is no more complicated than what we've described above. It is that simple ... and that challenging. It's also powerful and worth it. The key is to commit to sit every day, even if it's for five minutes. "One of my meditation teachers said that the most important moment in your meditation practice is the moment you sit down to do it. Because right then you're saying to yourself that you believe in change, you believe in caring for yourself, and you're making it real. You're not just holding some value like mindfulness or compassion in the abstract, but really making it real."

Recent research from neuroscientist Amishi Jha discovered that 12 minutes of meditation, 5 days a week can protect and strengthen your ability to pay attention.

Meditation Tips and Techniques

We've gone over the basic breath meditation so far, but there are other mindfulness techniques that use different focal points than the breath to anchor our attention—external objects like a sound in the room, or something broader, such as noticing spontaneous things that come into your awareness during an aimless wandering practice. But all of these practices have one thing in common: We notice that our minds ARE running the show a lot of the time. It's true. We think thoughts, typically, and then we act. But here are some helpful strategies to change that up:

How to Make Mindfulness a Habit

It's estimated that 95% of our behaviour runs on autopilot. That's because neural networks underlie all of our habits, reducing our millions of sensory inputs per second into manageable shortcuts so we can function in this crazy world. These default brain signals are so efficient that they often cause us to relapse into old behaviours before we remember what we meant to do instead.

Mindfulness is the exact opposite of these default processes. It's executive control rather than autopilot, and enables intentional actions, willpower, and decisions. But that takes practice. The more we activate the intentional brain, the stronger it gets. Every time we do something deliberate and new, we stimulate neuroplasticity, activating our grey matter, which is full of newly sprouted neurons that have not yet been groomed for "autopilot" brain.

But here's the problem. While our intentional brain knows what is best for us, our autopilot brain causes us to shortcut our way through life. So how can we trigger ourselves to be mindful when we need it most? This is where the notion of "behaviour design" comes in. It's a way to put your intentional brain in the driver's seat. There are two ways to do that—first, slowing down the autopilot brain by putting obstacles in its way, and second, removing obstacles in the path of the intentional brain, so it can gain control.

Shifting the balance to give your intentional brain more power takes some work, though. Here are some ways to get started.

• Put meditation reminders around you. If you intend to do some yoga or to meditate, put your yoga mat or your meditation cushion in the middle of your floor so you can't miss it as you walk by.

• Refresh your reminders regularly. Say you decide to use sticky notes to remind yourself of a new intention. That might work for about a week, but then your autopilot brain and old habits take over again. Try writing new notes to yourself; add variety or make them funny. That way they'll stick with you longer.

• Create new patterns. You could try a series of "If this, then that" messages to create easy reminders to shift into the intentional brain. For instance, you might come up with, "If office door, then deep breath," as a way to shift into mindfulness as you are about to start your workday. Or, "If phone rings, take a breath before answering." Each intentional action to shift into mindfulness will strengthen your intentional brain.

Meditating Practicing can help you to improve your mind power and increase your concentration power. make habits to do daily meditation at least 30 Minutes

CHAPTER NINE

Do Exercise Daily

Doing exercise will not help you in increasing mental stamina it will also help you to be healthy and feel energetic. Make habit to do daily morning exercise. It's better to don't join the gym do running in open garden will give you the best result as a compare to do workout in gym for mental health and fit body.

Whatever your age, there's strong scientific evidence that being physically active can help you lead a healthier and happier life. People who exercise regularly have a lower risk of developing many long-term (chronic) conditions, such as heart disease, type 2 diabetes, stroke, and some cancers

Exercise is defined as any movement that makes your muscles work and requires your body to burn calories. There are many types of physical activity, including swimming, running, jogging, walking, and dancing, to name a few. Being active has been shown to have many health benefits, both physically and mentally. It may even help you live long.

Exercise can make you feel happier

Exercising regularly can improve your mood and reduce feelings of anxiety and depression. Exercise has been shown to improve your mood and decrease feelings of depression, anxiety, and stress. It produces changes in the parts of the brain that regulate stress and anxiety. It can also increase brain sensitivity to the hormone's serotonin and norepinephrine, which relieve feelings of depression.

Exercise can increase the production of endorphins, which are known to help produce positive feelings and reduce the perception of pain.

Interestingly, it doesn't matter how intense your workout is. It seems that exercise can benefit your mood no matter the intensity of the physical activity.

In fact, in a study in 24 women diagnosed with depression, exercise of any intensity significantly decreased feelings of depression

The effects of exercise on mood are so powerful that choosing to exercise (or not) even makes a difference over short periods of time.

One review of 19 studies found that active people who stopped exercising regularly experienced significant increases in symptoms of depression and anxiety, even after only a few weeks.

Exercise can help with weight loss

Exercise is crucial to supporting a healthy metabolism and burning more calories per day. It also helps you maintain your muscle mass and weight loss.

Some studies have shown that inactivity is a major factor in weight gain and obesity

To understand the effect of exercise on weight reduction, it is important to understand the relationship between exercise and energy expenditure (spending).

Your body spends energy in three ways:

• digesting food

• exercising

• maintaining body functions,

like your heartbeat and breathing

While dieting, a reduced calorie intake will lower your metabolic rate, which can temporarily delay weight loss. On the contrary, regular exercise has been shown to increase your metabolic rate, which can burn more calories to help you lose weight.

Additionally, studies have shown that combining aerobic exercise with resistance training can maximize fat loss and muscle mass maintenance, which is essential for keeping the weight off and maintaining lean muscle mass.

Exercise is good for your muscles and bones

Physical activity helps you build muscles and strong bones. It may also help prevent osteoporosis.

Exercise plays a vital role in building and maintaining strong muscles and bones.

Activities like weightlifting can stimulate muscle building when paired with adequate protein intake.

This is because exercise helps release hormones that promote your muscles' ability to absorb amino acids. This helps them grow and reduces their breakdown.

As people age, they tend to lose muscle mass and function, which can lead to an increased risk of injury. Practicing regular physical activity is essential to reducing muscle loss and maintaining strength as you age.

Exercise also helps build bone density when you're younger, in addition to helping prevent osteoporosis later in life.

Exercise can increase your energy levels

Engaging in regular physical activity can increase your energy levels.

Exercise can be a real energy booster for many people, including those with various medical conditions.

One older study found that 6 weeks of regular exercise reduced feelings of fatigue for 36 people who had reported persistent fatigue.

And let's not forget the fantastic heart and lung health benefits of exercise. Aerobic exercise boosts the cardiovascular system and improves lung health, which can significantly help with energy levels.

As you move more, your heart pumps more blood, delivering more oxygen to your working muscles. With regular exercise, your heart becomes more efficient and adept at moving oxygen into your blood, making your muscles more efficient

Over time, this aerobic training results in less demand on your lungs, and it requires less energy to perform the same activities — one of the reasons you're less likely to get short of breath during vigorous activity.

Additionally, exercise has been shown to increase energy levels in people with other conditions, such as cancer.

Exercise can reduce your risk of chronic disease

Daily physical activity is essential to maintaining a healthy weight and reducing the risk of chronic disease.

Lack of regular physical activity is a primary cause of chronic disease.

Regular exercise has been shown to improve insulin sensitivity, heart health, and body composition. It can also decrease blood pressure and cholesterol levels.

More specifically, exercise can help reduce or prevent the following chronic health conditions.

• Type 2 diabetes. Regular aerobic exercise may delay or prevent type 2 diabetes. It also has considerable health benefits for people with type 1 diabetes. Resistance training for type 2 diabetes includes improvements in fat mass, blood pressure, lean body mass, insulin resistance, and glycemic control.

• Heart disease. Exercise reduces cardiovascular risk factors and is also a therapeutic treatment for people with cardiovascular disease.

• Many types of cancer. Exercise can help reduce the risk of several cancers, including breast, colorectal, endometrial, gallbladder, kidney, lung, liver, ovarian, pancreatic, prostate, thyroid, gastric, and esophageal cancer.

• High cholesterol. Regular moderate intensity physical activity can increase HDL (good) cholesterol while maintaining or offsetting increases in LDL (bad) cholesterol. Research supports the theory that high intensity aerobic activity is needed to lower LDL levels.

• Hypertension: Participating in regular aerobic exercise can lower resting systolic BP 5–7 mmHG among people with hypertension.

In contrast, a lack of regular exercise — even in the short term — can lead to significant increases in belly fat, which may increase the risk of type 2 diabetes and heart disease.

That's why regular physical activity is recommended to reduce belly fat and decrease the risk of developing these conditions.

Exercise can help skin health

Moderate exercise can provide antioxidant protection and promote blood flow, which can protect your skin and delay signs of aging.

Your skin can be affected by the amount of oxidative stress in your body.

Oxidative stress occurs when the body's antioxidant defences cannot completely repair the cell damage caused by compounds known as free radicals. This can damage the structure of the cells and negatively impact your skin.

Even though intense and exhaustive physical activity can contribute to oxidative damage, regular moderate exercise can actually increase your body's production of natural antioxidants, which help protect cells.

In the same way, exercise can stimulate blood flow and induce skin cell adaptations that can help delay the appearance of skin aging.

Exercise can help your brain health and memory

Regular exercise improves blood flow to the brain and helps brain health and memory. Among older adults, it can help protect mental function.

Exercise can improve brain function and protect memory and thinking skills.

To begin with, it increases your heart rate, which promotes the flow of blood and oxygen to your brain. It can also stimulate the production of hormones that enhance the growth of brain cells.

Plus, the ability of exercise to prevent chronic disease can translate into benefits for your brain, since its function can be affected by these conditions.

Regular physical activity is especially important in older adults since aging — combined with oxidative stress and inflammation — promotes changes in brain structure and function (38Trusted Source, 39Trusted Source).

Exercise has been shown to cause the hippocampus, a part of the brain that's vital for memory and learning, to grow in size, which may help improve mental function in older adults

Lastly, exercise has been shown to reduce changes in the brain that can contribute to conditions like Alzheimer's disease and dementia.

Exercise can help with relaxation and sleep quality

Regular physical activity, regardless of whether it is aerobic or a combination of aerobic and resistance training, can help you sleep better and feel more energized during the day.

Regular exercise can help you relax and sleep better.

With regard to sleep quality, the energy depletion (loss) that occurs during exercise stimulates restorative processes during sleep.

Moreover, the increase in body temperature that occurs during exercise is thought to improve sleep quality by helping body temperature drop during sleep.

Many studies on the effects of exercise on sleep have reached similar conclusions.

One review of six studies found that participating in an exercise training program helped improve self-reported sleep quality and reduced sleep latency, which is the amount of time it takes to fall asleep.

One study conducted over 4 months found that both stretching and resistance exercise led to improvements in sleep for people with chronic insomnia.

Getting back to sleep after waking, sleep duration, and sleep quality improved after both stretching and resistance exercise. Anxiety was also reduced in the stretching group.

What's more, engaging in regular exercise seems to benefit older adults, who are often affected by sleep disorders.

You can be flexible with the kind of exercise you choose. It appears that either aerobic exercise alone or aerobic exercise combined with resistance training can both improve sleep quality.

CHAPTER TEN

BE A GREAT PERSONALITY

How to be a great personality it can be learned it or can knowledge by any person. Personality is the typical pattern of thinking, feeling, and behaviours that make a person unique.

When we say that someone has a "good personality" we mean that they are likable, interesting and pleasant to be with.

In fact, approximately 85 percent of your success and happiness will be a result of how well you interact with others. Ultimately, it is your personality that determines whether people are attracted to, or shy away from you.

A person's personality shows a person past and futures. It can be predicted by seeing his gestures and postures. For improving personality person have to tack care of his gesture posture,

For improving your personality, you have to look good, you have to talk in good way, you have to sit, walk, eat in a very good way in a dissenting manner.

Read below things will help you to improve your personality.

1.Be honest with yourself, always.

Awkward situations are always uncomfortable. Don't try to be someone that you aren't. If you meet some new people don't worry about not having anything in common with them, just make light conversation, be friendly, and ask questions

2. Be Happy.

Try to always look on the bright side, be positive and smile. No one can resist a happy person. This doesn't mean be fake or feel you have to hide your feelings. If something's really bothering you, never feel you have to fake a smile. Just make sure you try to see the best in things and show people that you're a happy person

3.Show your confidence. You don't have to be someone you aren't, but confidence can take many forms. Being confident doesn't mean you have to suddenly be extremely extroverted and talkative. Reassure yourself every day that you are amazing. Just be confident in the personality that you have and other people will be drawn to you. There's no use faking it. People are attracted to those that are real.

4. Try to be nice

This is the most important step. No matter who you are, if you are nice, the only reason a person can dislike you is if they are jealous of you. Never be rude to people. If someone is being unkind to you, try to imagine what might be causing him or her to act this way. Maybe they are going through a really difficult situation in their life and in reality, they are a very good person. Try to assume the best in people. You don't have to be naïve and it's okay to remain sceptical, but that doesn't mean you ever have an excuse to treat anyone poorly

5.Remain cool, calm and collected.

You always have to remember to keep your cool. This will earn you an enormous amount of respects, especially if you keep calm in situations where everyone else panics. Just try to take things as they come and don't get too high or too low. This is something that you can do consciously and people will really respect your ability to keep everything together

6.Be a better listener.

Jacqueline Kennedy Onassis was considered one of the most charming women in the world because she cultivated the skill of being an exceptional listener. She was known for the way she would look a person in the eyes, hang on their every word, and make them feel important. There is nothing more appealing than having someone listen to you intently making you feel like you're the only person in the world.

7.Be a good conversationalist.

This relates to how much you read and know. Once you have much to contribute, learn how to talk about it with others. No one can read about or know everything, so it's refreshing to learn from others those things we don't have the time to about read ourselves.

8.Have a positive outlook and attitude.

Who wants to be around people who are negative, complain a lot, or have nothing good to say? In fact, most of us run when we see them coming. Instead, be the kind of upbeat person who lights up a room with your energy when you enter it. Do it by looking for the best in people and things. Smile warmly, spread good cheer, and enliven others with your presence.

9.Be fun and see the humorous side of life.

Everyone enjoys the company of someone who makes them laugh or smile, so look for the humorous, quirky side in a situation - there always is one. Comic relief is a much-welcome and needed diversion at times. When you can add fun and light-heartedness to an otherwise dull or gloomy setting, others will naturally be attracted to you, not to mention grateful.

10. Be supportive of others.

Being supportive is probably the most endearing quality you can integrate into your personality. Just as you welcome it, be the support for others when they need it. We all love a cheerleader in our corner; someone who is encouraging believes in us and helps pick us up when we're down.

CHAPTER ELEVEN

BE RICH OR MILLINEOR

If a person wants to win his friends, neighbours, and all the people of this world and wants to succeed in his life he should have a few qualities and characteristics.

I am sharing about the qualities and characteristics and some experience of great leaders and how they win on this planet and still are here in the form of their thoughts.

The first quality and characteristic a person should have to win the heart of people is the capability to become Rich. It does not matter about he is Rich or not he should have the qualities to Earn money and become famous. For that, he should learn the skills so he gets whatever he wants in his life and become successful in his life.

Wealth nearly everyone wants it, but few people actually know what they need to do in order to get it. Becoming rich takes a combination of luck, skill, and patience. To get rich, you'll need to set yourself on a path that leads to a monetarily enriching career, then handle the money you earn wisely by investing it, saving it, and reducing your living expenses. Getting rich isn't easy, but with a little bit of perseverance and skilful decision making, it's definitely possible.

Put money in the stock market. Invest money in stocks, bonds, or other vehicles of investment that will give you an annual return on investment (ROI) great enough to sustain you in your retirement. For instance, if you have one million dollars invested and you get a reliable 7% ROI, that's $70,000 per year, less inflation.

Don't get enticed by day traders who tell you it's easy to make a quick buck. Buying and selling dozens of stocks every day is essentially gambling. If you make some bad trades — which is unbelievably easy to do — you can lose a lot of money. It's not a good way to get rich.

Instead, learn to invest for the long run. Choose good stocks and passive funds with solid fundamentals and excellent leadership in industries that are primed for future growth. Then let your stock sit. Don't do anything with it. Let it weather the ups and downs. If you invest wisely, you should do very well over time.

If you're starting with a small amount of money to invest, index funds might be a good option for you, as they have low fees and can give you some relatively safe exposure to the stock market.

Save money for retirement. Keep saving. It seems that fewer people are saving adequately for retirement. Some feel they may never be able to retire. Take advantage of tax-deferred retirement plans such as IRAs and 401Ks. The tax treatment they embody will help you save faster for retirement.

Don't put all your trust in Social Security. While it's a good bet that Social Security will continue to work for the next 20 or so years, some data suggest that if Congress doesn't radically alter the system — either by raising taxes or reducing benefits — Social Security won't be available in its current form. It is probable, however, that Congress will act to "fix" Social Security. In any event, Social Security was never designed to be the only resource for retirees in their later years. That makes it all the more important that you save and invest for the future.

Invest in a Roth IRA. A Roth IRA is a retirement account to which working individuals can contribute an annual sum of $5,500. That money is then invested and gathers compound interest. If you wait until retirement age to take money out of your Roth IRA, the money that you withdraw isn't taxed, because it was taxed at the time you first earned it.

Contribute to EPF account. This is an account set up by your employer where pre-taxed contributions ca n be invested. Your employer may choose to match all or part of your contributions. This is probably the closest thing you'll get to "free money" in your life! Contribute at least enough to take full advantage of the match

Invest in real estate. Relatively stable assets like rental properties, or potential development land in a steadily growing area is a good way to build wealth. As with any investment, there are no guarantees. Many people, however, have done quite well with real estate. Such investments are likely to appreciate in value over time. For example, some people think that an apartment in Manhattan is almost guaranteed to increase in value over any five-year period.

Excel academically. Whether it's a four-year college or vocational training, some successful people pursue further education beyond high school. In the early stages of a career, your employers have little by which to judge you besides your educational background. Higher grades usually lead to higher salaries.

Choose the right profession. Look at salary surveys which indicate average annual incomes for specific professions. Your odds of getting rich are diminished if you pursue a career in teaching as opposed to a career in finance. Here are some of the highest paying jobs in America:

Doctors and surgeons. Anaesthesiologists make a whopping $200,000+ per year.

Petroleum engineers. Engineers who work with gas and oil companies can make a very good living. In most cases, they make upwards of $135,000 per year.

Attorneys. Lawyers top out at just above $130,000 per year, making this a lucrative field if you can put in the time.

IT managers and software engineers. If you're good at programming and a whiz at computers, consider this very well-compensated field. IT managers regularly make $125,000 per year.

Choose the right location. Go where the good jobs are. If you want to pursue finance, for example, there are far greater opportunities in big cities than in rural, low-populated areas. If you want to build a start-up, you'll probably want to consider going to Silicon Valley. If you want to make it big in the entertainment industry, go to that place.

Change jobs and employer. Once you've gotten some experience under your belt, consider finding a new job. By changing your environment, you can increase your pay and experience different corporate cultures. Don't be afraid to do this several times. If you're a valued employee, it's also likely your current company may offer you a raise or other benefits if they know you're looking at leaving.

Make a budget (and stick to it). Create a monthly budget that covers all of your basic expenses and leaves a little bit of "fun" money aside. Sticking by your budget and saving at least some money each month is a good way to lay the groundwork for your efforts to get rich.

Skill is very important for becoming a successful man and living a healthy life. I am describing below skills that can help him.

Track down your expenses. To soar your efficiency on cutting your expenses, it is vital to keep track of them. Pick one of the numerous expense tracking applications there are around, like Money Lover or Mint, and record every single penny that goes in and out of your wallet. After 3 months or so, you should be able to know where most of your money go and what can you do for that.

Break up with your credit card. Did you know that people who use credit cards for purchases end up spending more money than people who use cash? That's because parting with cash is painful. Using a credit card doesn't carry that much of a sting. If you can, divorce your credit card and see how it feels to pay with cash. You'll probably end up saving a boatload of money.

If you do maintain a credit card, do things to reduce expenses. Try to pay off the full balance each month and on time. That results in interest-free credit. At the very least, make the monthly minimum payment before the due date to avoid a late fee.

1. Communication skills- Developing strong communication skills is essential when it comes to building a successful career. But your communication skills play a key role in your private life too. Learn about the most in-demand communication skills and how to improve them. Successful communication helps us better understand people and situations. It helps us overcome diversities, build trust and respect, and create conditions for sharing creative ideas and solving problems. A person should have communication skills that can help him to succeed in life, and he can improve them. practicing in front of a mirror or in front of animals is a very good way to improve your skills. if someone wants to join any coaching classes or institute that will also help them but still, he has to do continuously practice on that.

2. Continuity- For learning any skill or knowledge man has to continue the practice of that without any excuse.

3. Understand the value of Time- The value of time is not learned by reading books. One can only understand it by practicing good habits to lead a disciplined life. We have all heard our elders saying that time waits for none; stop procrastinating and do your assigned job within the given time frame. Everyone emphasizes the value of time, so you understand how much it matters. Time slips away from your hand like sand; you cannot hold it forever. It flies by. Time is finite but also infinite. Time is the most treasured thing in our lives that makes us disciplined and helps us lead a good life. Wastage of time can hamper our growth and success. We must use our time efficiently to excel in life.

A Person should understand the value of qualities like time is money and everything you have to feel that things. without feelings. you can't understand the value of time. due to a single second, a person can die. There are many examples are there which says if a person not use the time he will definitely fail in his life

4. Feel the situation – A person should feel everything that he is doing. He is doing wrong or right or doing good or bad. If he is not aware of all things, he will do a great mistake which he will pay a big price on the future.

Learn Deep Skills- Each person should learn deep skills a person should be an expert in one subject. For that, he can do studied daily her subject.

Make Passive income- For becoming Rich and successful person man have to earn money form various way. With a passive income stream, you can earn money over time with little to no sustained effort. Here are some ideas to get started. Passive income is a money stream that requires little or no continuous effort. As a business model, it's largely self-sustaining; often, passive income involves some kind of upfront or initial investment that generates long-term steady gains. the Internal Revenue Service (IRS) defines two "passive activities

1. Trade or business activities that don't require material participation.
2. Rental activities.

Earning passive income can be an enticing idea, but it's important to note that it can take some time to grow your investments

Passive income ideas

Make financial investments

Financial investments include a range of options, such as investing in the stock market, mutual funds, bonds, and peer lending, and they require minor follow-up work as they accrue interest. Work with a financial advisor to figure out the best investment options for you.

2. Own a rental property.

Rental income can be a steady way to earn extra money, but, whether you house long-term tenants or short-term renters, this passive income source comes with all the required maintenance of regular home ownership.

Self publishing

If you have a wealth of knowledge or an idea for a story, you can write a book and sell it online. Many people choose to use a service like Kindle Direct Publishing, which enables you to transform your words into an ebook or print edition and sell it on Amazon.

Create content.

If video is your medium of choice, you can earn money by uploading your original creations to YouTube and setting your account up for monetization with the YouTube Partner Program. There's no limit to the types of videos you can create—informational, short film, original music, even ambient noise—however there are a number of requirements to join the YouTube Partner Program, including a minimum number of views and followers.

And many more ideas is there which can help you be Rich.

I want to give the definition of success according to our great leaders who get success on this planet. They things success means living a happy life and making a society where all human beings as well as other creatures live happily.

But before making any YouTube channel should read the term and conditions so your channel will not be deleted due to that.

You do a lot hard work to grow your channel and suddenly YouTube suspend it then you not get anything and its be just wasting your time.

So be very careful on doing these

CHAPTER TWELVE

LIVE DICIPLINED LIFE

The first and best victory is to conquer self

Discipline is not obedience to someone else's standards to avoid punishment. It is learning and applying intentional standards to achieve meaningful objectives.

Learning to effectively lead yourself and others all comes down to discipline. Happiness, success, and fulfilment stem from focus and self-control. It may be hard to believe when you're facing an all-you-can-eat buffet, the prospect of making a quick buck, or the lazy lure of sleeping in versus getting on the Peloton, but studies show that people with self-discipline are happier. Why? Because with discipline and self-control we actually accomplish more of the goals we truly care about. Self-discipline is the bridge between goals defined and goals accomplished.

I am just sharing a story which is shows how discipline is the Key of success.

Three young men were going through the woods on a bright sunny day.

These men were wonderful buddies, and they all had ambitious goals in life. John, Kevin, and Frank were their names.

As the friends were chatting about their goals, talking about pretty girls, and cracking jokes, Kevin suddenly fell into the Earth with a yelp!

John and Frank ran over to the hole where Kevin fell.

John yelled, "Oh my gosh Kevin! Are you okay?"

Kevin replied weakly, "Yeah, I think so... can you guys help me get out of here?"

Frank and John grabbed Kevin and pulled him up.

"Thanks, guys, I thought I was a goner for a second there. What is this hole?"

Frank pulled out a pocket flashlight and shined the light down the hole.

"I think it's a well," said Frank.

John muttered, "Well jeez, I saw a danger warning sign or something was telling you that there was a well smack dab in the middle of the forest path."

Suddenly, a sign appeared in front of the three friends that read, "DANGER! Magical Well Ahead. Watch your step!"

Frank, John, and Kevin were flabbergasted. They could not believe their eyes.

Kevin exclaimed, "No way! This has got to be a dream. So basically, this is a real-life wishing well? I thought this stuff only happened in the movies."

The other two friends murmured in agreement.

Frank decided to take a chance of looking like a fool and wished for an apple.

An apple appeared in front of them out of nowhere.

When the other two buddies realised what was going on, they made their wishes as well.

Kevin wants a gorgeous lady to take out on a date, while John wishes for a new bicycle.

A black gear bicycle and a lovely young woman emerged out of nowhere.

Frank stood passively watching as John rode around on his new bicycle while Kevin struck up a flirting chat with his new girlfriend. He could tell something wasn't quite right.

His father had always warned him that if something seemed too good to be true, it was most likely true.

By wishing in a well, no one gets anything for nothing. There had to be a catch, Frank thought.

Just as that thought bubbled up in his mind, John yelled as he crashed into the bushes while riding the cycle.

The bike had disappeared out from underneath him! Kevin's new lady friend also disappeared into thin air, which left him disappointed as things were coming along quite well for him up until that moment.

"What the heck happened? My new bike vanished!" exclaimed John.

Frank checked his watch.

"Guys, you've been making your wishes for exactly 30 minutes. I believe you should try again in 30 minutes and see if it happens again."

John and Kevin made their same respective wishes again. This time, nothing happened.

"Maybe we can't make the same wish twice or something? I wish for a sports car!" said John.

Almost instantly, a shiny red Ferrari appeared before him.

"Sweet!" said John.

Feeling depressed about losing his new girlfriend, Kevin wished for his favourite junk food, sat down, and started eating.

Again, Frank wished for nothing more, wanting to see what would happen again after 30 minutes.

Lo-and-behold, in another 30 minutes John fell to the ground and gained a few scratches and bruises.

Luckily, the Ferrari was parked when the 30 minutes were up! John had just been sitting inside.

After making sure his friend was okay, Frank turned to Kevin and asked, "Kevin, does your stomach feel any lighter?"

"No, I can still feel the food in my stomach," Kevin said, having long since finished his dinner. I suppose if you eat whatever you want before the 30 minutes are over, you get to keep it!"

The three pals would return to the well together over the next few weeks.

Kevin and John wished for more and more things that they've always wanted but didn't feel they could get without the magic of the well.

Frank did end up making a few wishes and had some fun, but quickly grew dissatisfied.

He accompanied the other two friends less frequently as time passed.

Frank observed that his friends stopped talking about their goals and plans for the future as much as they had in the past.

Now, all they could think about was what they were going to wish for next from the magical well.

As time went on, Frank grew more distant from Kevin and John.

Noticing this Kevin and John confronted Frank and asked him why he was spending less time with them.

"You folks think this well is a wonderful treasure," Frank explained, "but all I see is fool's gold." None of the things we wish for here endures very long, and I believe you're beginning to get addicted. Plus, if you don't work for what you have, you won't appreciate it as much, and you won't take enough breaks from the nonstop indulgence."

Kevin, who had acquired weight as a result of all the food he had requested, responded, "Fine then." Max, you're free to do as you choose. We don't need you or your stuffy principles as long as we have this magical well here."

John nodded. "We have everything we need," says the narrator. Sure, it doesn't last very long, but we may keep hoping for things and never have to deal with the stress of hard work. Why put up the effort if you don't have to?"

Frank tried to warn his friends of the hidden dangers of the magic well, but they refused to listen.

At that moment, Frank bid his lifelong friends farewell, as there was nothing more he could do to convince them.

He began walking away, all alone.

For the next couple of decades, Frank went to work.

His mastery of discipline allowed him to have complete control over himself and his appetites.

Although he was a very successful and influential man who could have nearly anything he wanted, have a beautiful house, cars but he rarely over-indulged himself.

He enjoyed incredible experiences that came with his wealth, but he did so in moderation, balancing pleasure with disciplined effort.

One morning, Frank found himself feeling guilty.

On a sunny day, he was in his backyard, overlooking a beautiful blue ocean sea, with his gleaming white house proudly standing behind him.

He was thinking about his friends from all those years ago as he gazed into the water.

He felt like he'd abandoned them, so he decided to go to the woods.

He knew he'd have to wait a long time for them to come around to the magical well because he didn't know if they still lived near it or even if they still frequented it as frequently as they used to.

Despite this, he packed his camping gear and drove to the woods. He carefully stepped onto the route after parking his red Bentley SUV outside the trees.

Suddenly, an old-looking man with a long beard and dark eye bags under his eyes appeared from the bushes.

He was smelly, extremely skinny, dirty-looking, and seemed to be wearing rags.

"M-Frank?" whimpered John.

At Frank appeared confused, but then his expression quickly changed to one of pure horror. "Oh my god, John, is that you?"

After a tense conversation with John, Frank discovered that John and Kevin had moved into the woods to be closer to the well several decades ago.

They'd become completely entangled with what it could do for them.

The longer they stayed with the well, the more dependent they became on it.

Since everything they wished for disappeared in 30 minutes, they had nothing to show for the years they spent in the woods, which was in complete contrast to Frank.

Not only that, but they never acquired key virtues like patience, diligence, gratitude, and discipline because they never had to labour for what the well gave.

The magic well sent both Kevin and John into a downward spiral of self-destruction for many years.

Unfortunately, John informed Frank that Kevin had passed away many years ago from complications caused by all the unhealthy food and drink he addictively wished for.

John did not know how to cope with the loss of his friend and felt that he couldn't integrate himself back into society, so he decided to live out the rest of his life in the woods.

Over the years, John had grown tired of wishing for things that only destroyed his body and mind further.

He began to wish for tools and nature literature from the well to learn how to live off the land naturally and be free of its terrifying influence.

Frank and John spent the rest of the day together catching up, although it wasn't exactly a joyous reunion.

At the end of the day, Frank invited John to come to stay with him until he could transition back into society, but John vehemently refused.

As Frank turned to leave and return home, John called, "You were right you know. All those years ago, you tried to warn us, Frank. Like fools, we tried to take immediate gratification without putting in the discipline to create truly lasting rewards in our lives. I realize it now. If we had listened, maybe Kevin would still be with us."

Frank froze after hearing John's words. Unsure of what to say, Frank continued walking towards his car with tears rolling down his face.

The conclusion of the story is that nothing worthwhile in life is possible without self-discipline.

In our own lives, the "magic well" might take numerous shapes.

For some, it may emerge as a never-ending search for a "get-rich-quick" scheme.

It could be an addiction to television, video games, or partying for others.

For others, it could be chasing the opposite sex all the time.

All of these things, like Frank, Kevin, and John's storey, might provide instant gratification, but they are all fleeting and ephemeral.

If you want to be truly successful, you must eliminate all "magic wells" in your life and devote yourself to the development of self-discipline via actual practice.

There is no other option.

There is another great teaching form Bhagbat Gita,

There Arujuna asked to lord krishna

चञ्चल हि मन: कृष्ण प्रमाथि बलवद्दृढम् |

तस्याह निग्रिह मन्ये वायोरवि सदुष्करम् ||

Translation: The mind is very restless, turbulent, strong and obstinate, O Krishna. It appears to me that it is more difficult to control than the wind.

It is true that one who has controlled his mind can attain anything in his life. But our mind is most of the time unsteady, uncooperative, and restless.

Arjuna goes to the extent of saying that if you instruct me, I will conquer all the enemies. If you order me, I can even control the wind. But if you tell me to control the mind then it won't be possible.

"The mind is restless, turbulent, obstinate and very strong, O Krishna, and to subdue it, I think, is more difficult than controlling the wind."

We are completely helpless in front of our mind. Just like a lamb is helpless in front of the tiger.

Many yogis and mystics have tried in the past to gain control over their mind, but they failed. Sage Viswamitra renounced everything, retired to the forest, and did penance(tapasya) for several years. But he too failed to control his mind. As soon as he saw Menaka, he could not resist himself and got allured.

There are innumerable such examples. Even great personalities face so difficulty in controlling the mind.

You suffer because of your uncontrolled mind

You and I too face so many challenges in life because of our restless mind. Whether it be your personal life or professional life, you face difficulties because your mind does not allow you to act wisely. It compels you to indulge in certain activities for which you regret later.

You easily get distracted because of your uncontrolled mind.

Your restless mind does not allow you to focus on your work.

A student knows that if he studies hard, he will get good grades. But as soon as he opens his books within few minutes his mind takes him to some other world. His attention span is so short.

This is why we see many students who may be sitting with their books for hours but does not get good grades. Because they never studied.

Working professionals too face similar problem. You may be sitting at your work desk trying to complete your task, but you are not able to focus. It is not that you do not know how to do your work, but your mind does not allow you to concentrate. You are not able to sit for long hours and work. You easily get distracted.

After every few minutes, you begin checking your emails knowing very well that no important email is going to come. But you check because you are not able to focus on your task.

Again, you start working but after few minutes you start browsing internet. You look for some breaking news. You again and again check Facebook, Twitter, and WhatsApp. You take breaks which are not required. You chitchat with colleagues to kill time.

So, a piece of work which you could have easily completed with few hours of focussed work, you take several hours or even days to complete it.

Just before an important meeting you frantically try to complete your presentation or status report. It is only after repeated reminder emails that you complete internal trainings. You keep on procrastinating.

You do not work proactively. You work only when an external force is applied. Just like a horse does not pull the cart unless it is whipped.

It is not because of lack of knowledge or talent that you do not grow in your professional life. But it is due to lack of self-discipline and commitment.

You remain mediocre because your mind remains distracted. It always overpowers you.

Advice Lord Krishna gives in Bhagavad Gita to control the mind:

Arjuna, 5000 years ago was facing similar problem. Arjuna was not an ordinary personality. He was a formidable warrior. The best archer of his time. He had defeated many enemies. Had won many battles. But he too appeared helpless in front of his mind.

Krishna completely agreed with Arjuna. He too said that controlling mind is indeed difficult.

But he did not stop there. He immediately said that "It is not impossible!"

Krishna gave Arjuna hope. In fact, he is giving hope to you and me.

Arjuna is not asking questions for himself only. He knew that everyone in this world face similar challenges. So, he is asking questions on behalf of you and me.

And Krishna is not answering only to Arjuna. But he is even answering to us.

He is asking us not to get disheartened. He is assuring us that there is a way by which we can control our restless mind.

Lord Shri Krishna says to Arjuna, "O mighty-armed son of Kunti, it is undoubtedly very difficult to curb the restless mind, but it is possible by suitable practice and by detachment."

So, he recommends two process:

1. Practice

2. Detachment

Controlling the mind by practice (abhyasena)

Practice means to do something repeatedly till we become proficient.

For example, when a child for the first time tries to ride a bicycle, he falls. He may start thinking that it is impossible for him to ride a bicycle. During the process of learning he fails many times. But by trying again and again he learns the skill. He then fearlessly enjoys his bicycle ride.

It is true that controlling mind is more difficult than learning a bicycle.

But think when you were a child. You also initially thought riding a bicycle is impossible. You envied when you saw your elder brother or sister riding the cycle. You desperately wanted to be like them. And one day you succeeded.

Similarly, with practice you should try your best to gain control over your mind.

When you were a kid, you had enthusiasm. You had hope. You had a strong desire to learn something new. Now when you grow old, you lack enthusiasm, hope and a desire to take up challenges.

But you need to nurture childlike enthusiasm. You should have hope in the words of Krishna. And a strong desire to subdue the mind.

What practice to do to control the mind?

You should practice focusing the mind on the activities you are doing currently. You should not allow the mind to get distracted. You should bring back the mind to the present state as soon as it wanders.

Will you succeed immediately. Definitely Not. Will you fail initially. Definitely Yes.

But you have to keep on trying.

And by repeated practice, you will ultimately attain victory over your mind.

The great Vedic sages practiced meditation to control the mind.

They meditated on the holy names and transcendental forms of the Lord. When their mind got distracted, they would force their mind to focus on their object of meditation.

Mantra meditation is the best way to gain control over your mind

In the present age mantra meditation is the recommended process to gain control over our restless mind.

You should chant the holy names of Krishna. While chanting you should focus on the words of the Mahamantra (Hare, Krishna & Rama) and simultaneously try to hear the transcendental sound.

We all who chant the Hare Krishna Mahamantra have the experience that during chanting, our mind wanders many times. It is not unexpected.

But immediately we should bring back the mind from wherever it has gone and focus on chanting.

Initially when one starts chanting, mind wanders frequently. I remember during my college days when first time I held the beads in my hand and began chanting it was impossible to chant. I was not even able to chant for 5 minutes.

But by constant practice today I can chant for around 2 hours daily.

It takes several years of repeated practice to attain complete control over the mind. But during your initial days also, you will experience that you are in a much better situation. The mind is now not wandering a lot.

How detachment (Vairagya) helps to gain control over the mind?

Vairagya or detachment means freeing your mind from those material activities which is harmful for the mind. When your mind associates with matter it becomes impure. And an impure mind troubles a lot.

So, you should not expose your mind to those environments which aggravates lust, anger, and greed.

But you should always expose your mind to such environment where it becomes peaceful and calm. Where it gets filled with positivity.

And a controlled mind becomes your best friend. You are then able to accomplish great results.

Controlling mind is a herculean task. But by following the formula given by Krishna in Bhagavad Gita, you can gain control over your mind. Krishna is teaching that by practice and detachment it is possible to control the mind. And a controlled mind will become your best friend.

Once your mind becomes your best friend, it will assist you in whatever activities you will do.

If you are a student, then you will be able to study hard with single minded attention. You will no longer face failure but will always get very good grades in exam.

If you are a working professional then you will be able to do your work with sincerity, with complete attention. You won't get distracted. You will be able to complete your work in time and even before time. No last minute hurry. No stress. No fear of being reprimanded by the boss. No fear of being laid off because of poor performance.

Theodore Roosevelt once said, "With self-discipline, almost anything is possible." Self-discipline is, indeed, regarded as one of the keys to success. Many people attribute self-discipline as having determination and fortitude. That means having the strength and will to continue carrying out what one wants to achieve despite setbacks and hardships. But in actual fact, self-discipline is more about having self-control or the ability to control your desires and not falling prey to bad habits, such as laziness, procrastination and irresponsibility. In other words, self-discipline is having the willpower to fight your wilful desires.

When a teenager gets up early and prepares him/herself for online classes, that is self-discipline, as they resist the desire to sleep longer. If a student turns off his/her mobile phone to study peacefully without any distraction, that is self-discipline. Making great efforts to abstain from bad habits, such as smoking or too much gaming, is also self-discipline. So, basically, self-discipline is regulating yourself for the sake of improvement or betterment of your situation.

Self-discipline is something difficult to achieve, since it really requires one to battle with one's own self in making the right choice. But true self-discipline is not punishing oneself and it is not supposed to restrict a person's lifestyle or the right for some leisure. It is to make the right choice at the right time when the time calls for it. Like completing your assignment first before playing games. It actually denotes one's mental and inner strength, which is crucial in leading a more meaningful life. Self-discipline grants you freedom - freedom from being a slave to your wilful desires and wants. It helps you to divide your time wisely between study/ work, rest and entertainment.

Self-discipline delays short-term gratification for long-term reward

Having self-discipline helps us to overcome laziness and procrastination and prevents us from taking things for granted. It directs us to choose what we want now and what we want for the future. Maxwell Maltz, author of a self-help book called "Psycho-Cybernetics: A New Way to Get More Living out of Life", said, "The ability to discipline yourself to delay gratification in the short term in order to enjoy greater rewards in the long term is the indispensable prerequisite for success". Self-discipline makes you re-evaluate what you need to do now in order to achieve success in the future. As the saying goes, what you sow now is what you will reap in the future.

The self-disciplined person takes control of his own life

Having self-discipline helps us to overcome laziness and procrastination and prevents us from taking things for granted. It directs us to choose what we want now and what we want for the future. Maxwell Maltz, author of a self-help book called "Psycho-Cybernetics: A New Way to Get More Living out of Life", said, "The ability to discipline yourself to delay gratification in the short term in order to enjoy greater rewards in the long term is the indispensable prerequisite for success". Self-discipline makes you re-evaluate what you need to do now in order to achieve success in the future. As the saying goes, what you sow now is what you will reap in the future.

You alone are responsible for your quality of life

One thing about self-discipline is that it is a learned skill, not something innate. Some people are taught self-discipline when they are young, like making their own beds, having salad at every meal or having a specific time for study and play, while others do not. But, however you were brought up, it is never too late to learn self-discipline. All you need is a strategy and a little practice. Some strategies that you can employ to increase your self-discipline are, for example, establishing a daily routine, like sleeping and getting up at the same time every day, having a specific timetable for your daily activities and removing distractions and temptations slowly but consistently. Another good strategy is reminding yourself of the benefits of what you need to do compared to what you want to do.

Instilling self-discipline in yourself is not a walk in the park. It is challenging and many people fail. But this is where your determination and fortitude come in. Suffer the pain of self-discipline or you will suffer the pain of regret. Persevere and continue practicing self-discipline every day, and one day you will reap the fruits of your success.

"The best day of your life is the one on which you decide your life is your own. No apologies or excuses. No one to lean on, rely on, or blame. You alone are responsible for the quality of it." (Anon.)

6 Reasons Why Self Discipline Is Important For Success

Self-discipline is the key to success in life. You cannot succeed in life without it. Successful people will always suggest you to stay discipline. But the question is "why self-discipline is important for success in life"?

Self-discipline helps you to become unstoppable force of energy to reach greatest level in your life.

If you want to become successful in life, the first thing you need to do is discipline yourself.

Let's get to know 6 Reasons Why Self Discipline Is Important For Success.

1. Self-discipline creates a habit.

Habits can make you or break you. Self-discipline creates a habit in your life that builds up only through discipline.

Most people never remain disciplined in their lives because they are lazy. However, laziness is form of habit as well.

Successful people discipline themselves to work and stay consistent to it. And it becomes a habit. This is what attracts success in their lives.

Here are 5 best ways to turn your bad habits into good habits.

2. It helps you get things done.

Self-discipline is important to get things done. It can be anything, either you commit to read books or complete a task in a timeline.

When you discipline yourself to finish every single thing, you form a personality around it.

This habit makes you an achiever in your life.

Self-discipline is important for success. Because it helps you to remain consistent in life and when you're consistent, you will achieve anything you want in life.

3. It helps you to focus.

We live in a world full of distractions. Self-discipline helps you to focus on your goals. It helps you stick to the work you want to get it done in order to achieve success.

When you are focused on your goal, you will complete every single thing that needs to be done.

Successful people have laser sharp focus.

They are always looking forward towards their goals and achievements in life. This helps them achieve great level of success in their lives. Focus is important for self-discipline and if you want to be successful, you need to focus.

4. It boosts your self-esteem and work ethic.

Success comes to those who believe in themselves and who's the hardest worker in the room. Self-discipline helps you to boost your self-esteem and work ethic at the same time.

When you discipline yourself, you are actually improving your work ethic by sticking to it.

It will help you to achieve your objectives.

However, when you complete your objectives every day, you will start to boost your self-esteem and confidence in your work.

This is the reason self-discipline is important for success.

5. It helps you to achieve mastery.

Success comes to those who are masters not beginners. If you want success, you need to be master at something.

You become master by putting the work and spending upto 10,000 hours on one thing.

Mastery comes with discipline. Most people fail because they don't master anything. Whereas, successful people do one thing and master it.

So, this is how self-discipline will bring out mastery and mastery will bring out success.

6. It helps you to become best version of yourself.

Success comes only when you deserve it. You cannot become successful with the personality you currently have. So, you need improvements every single day. You need become best version of yourself to become successful in life.

Self-discipline helps you to improve yourself daily. When you do something consistently, you become better and better every day. So, this is why self-discipline is important for success and growth in life.

Self-discipline is the most important part of success. If you want to be successful in life, you need to have discipline. Otherwise, you will be knocked out by the people who are disciplined.

You have unlimited potential to reach greatest level in your life. All you need is self-discipline.

So why wasting time, go and start doing things that will take you closer to your goals in life.

CHAPTER THIRTEEN

DO WISH AND ACHIEVE IT

I have many wishes. I pray that some of them may come true. out of all the wishes, three are most important for me.

My first wish is to have a pencil that will turn everything that I draw, into real things. I would make so many things with that pencil. I would make chocolate and new clothes whenever I want and I would wear new clothes every day. I would make a bicycle and a lot of toys. I would also ask other people what they want and I would draw those things and give it to them.

My second wish is to fly like a bird. I love birds because they can fly when they want and they go wherever they want to go. Birds are free to fly and they are not like Aeroplanes and Kites. These things fly for only some time. Birds are independent. My favourite is the Eagle bird. It can fly very high in the sky. I wish I could become like it so that I could travel the whole world. I would see my city from above. I would love to fly in the clouds. There would be no noise there.

My third wish is to help poor people. I wish I could get lots of money in a big bag one day. I would take the money and give it to the poor people who ask for money on the roads. I would buy clothes and food for them. I would buy toys for children and they would play with them. They will be very happy and their parents will not be sad anymore.

My mother says that If I will study well, I would make them come true in some ways in my future.

If you want to achieve something, you have to make it happen without depending on anyone else to do it for you. "There is a light inside of every one of us, an ember that burns and begs us to become more than we have ever been. This is flicker of creativity, the spark of an idea.

If you want to achieve something, you have to make it happen without depending on anyone else to do it for you. "Every day the clock is ticking, every year the calender moves. Your 'IT' cannot be delayed forever. 'IT' is your dreams, your purpose,".

There are three types of people in this world, those who watch things happen, those who wonder what happened and those who make things happen. "You have got to determine which person you are. You could make a wish or you could make it happen. You must first believe that you can, that you will and that you must,"

Most of our wishes and dreams tend to be that way due to one key reason: belief.

But what if our dreams and wishes weren't really dreams in the first place and that everything, we could ever imagine could in fact come true?

Our lives can at times be quite confusing and at times, exciting, depending on how you choose to look at it. But one thing that's certain is that we are in control of everything we choose to experience in our lives, baring worldly and natural disasters.

The hard part is actually believing it and convincing ourselves that we can change our lives for the better.

Here are 12 tips to help you make the shift.

1) Pretend that you're already successful.

What do you really need to do to see yourself as a successful person? If you feel you have to achieve or be something in order to become it, then chances are, you will be waiting forever.

The truth is: success has no prerequisite and can only be given and assigned to the person who doesn't think too much about it.

Have a belief with full conviction that success is something you were naturally born with and that success in itself is a by-product of everything you do. Which in reality, it is. All you have to do is think back at everything you've ever achieved in your life and you'll begin to realize the truth.

Whether it's succeeding at passing your exams or being lazy in front of the television with a tub of ice-cream, success is constantly around you.

2) Believing that you're successful isn't necessary.

Similar to #1, you don't need to convince yourself that you're successful in order to get started. If you look back on all the times where you failed at the things you were doing, you'll realize that it didn't really stop you from continuing to do it, simply because you had fun while doing it.

Focus more on the activity and its enjoyment and less on the success part, because your achievement will simply be a process of what you do and who you are. Don't struggle or work for it, for it will come in time eventually

Lord Krishna also said in bhagbat geeta . only doing is on your hand not the result. He said to do work and achieve the mastery in your skills never think about result. If you think about result then you will be not able to focus on your work. And defiantly then you will not get the success.

3) Set goals that are larger than you ever thought possible.

While setting goals is important, they very rarely stay constant due to consistently growing and maturing over a period of time. What I hoped to achieve at 19 is hardly similar to what I want to achieve now that I'm 29. But what has become clear over the years is that I've gained clarity on why I'm on this planet. I have a purpose now that I've aligned myself to it, which is forcing me to take action.

What's your purpose? Discover what it is and if you don't have one, spend every waking moment searching deep inside yourself until you find it. Most of the time, it's constantly staring at you in the face.

If what you do excites you, then it's a hint that you're on a right track.

4) Become interested in and conscious of your personal development.

When I look back at myself over the years and watch videos of myself talking and communicating, I realize just how far I've developed and how much I've acquired over the years. And this was back when I had no clue about personal development or self-help.

In short, it excites me just to see where I'll be in the next 10 years having now become conscious of it. You now have a choice as to which direction you want to go. This includes the choices you make, what type of personality you want to develop and the type of person you ultimately wish to become.

Nothing is left to chance and is all down to the decisions you make. It all starts now.

5) Focus on what needs to be done for that moment.

Whatever grand vision you have of yourself, realize that you can only achieve it by taking small baby steps towards it. No one ever got there by taking massive strides or within just a few days.

Have a realistic plan of action and focus on what needs to be done in that particular moment. It's pretty intuitive once you get the hang of it. Think about what you're doing and then ask yourself whether what you're doing is going to lead you to your ultimate goal. If it doesn't, then change your decision or if it does, continue.

6) Do things for the right reasons and not for the wrong reasons.

Always have a healthy reason as to why you want to be what it is you want to be.

Is being a movie star or a musician a way to finally gain the approval of people and women in order to finally see yourself as attractive? Or are you doing it because of your love for music and your passion and dedication to adding value to the craft?

Understand that succeeding at something in order to cover up wounds from the past won't clear them or make them better. The important thing is to firstly accept your past as a learning experience and to move on from it. Because the reality of it is, whether you succeed or fail, no one really cares. All that matters is how you value yourself, because no one else will see you in quite the same way as you will.

7) Track your mindsets and make notes on everything you do.

Always monitor your thoughts and feelings because they tend to get you off track if you're not careful of it. It's normal to feel down at times but if you let it go out of hand, it can affect your progress moving forward.

Learn to write down your thoughts and feelings on a notepad. Or better yet, write it in a diary and use it to deposit whatever's on your mind. It will help you find clarity with where ever you currently are and provide you with perspective, which will aid you with making progress.

8) Become conscious of your learning.

Similar to point #7, you have to always be willing to grow and improve on a daily basis. You can only really ever do this by keeping an open mind and reading up on whatever material you can get your hands on.

Sometimes, gaining access to mentors isn't possible. But it's never a bad idea to reach out to them via books, courses or audio products.

Make a decision on what you need to learn in order to get to where you want to go and seek to acquire them from in as many ways as possible.

9) Share your experiences with others.

There's simply no way a person can ever be happy or satisfied without sharing their lives with others. We're designed to be social creatures and as such, gain tremendous satisfaction with spending time with others who share the same values and interests as us.

Whether it's through friends or family, always share your thoughts, ideas and ambitions with people as it will help you feel less lonely.

10) Embrace your failures and frustrations along the way.

I firmly believe that life itself is a series of failures, which we need to experience in order to become better. There isn't a single person I've ever met on this planet who never managed to make any mistakes before they became successful.

It simply doesn't make sense for life to lack failures, else each person would have been born with everything they ever wanted to begin with. In truth, it's the failure that's the journey.

11) Learn to remain humble and down to earth.

Through failure, you'll get to develop an appreciation for what you eventually have in your life due to the hardships you had to deal with in order to get there.

I don't know a single person who appreciated what they had when it was given to them easily versus when they had to work hard for it. At the end of the day, you owe it to yourself to work hard for what you want out of your life.

Because it's what will help you appreciate it and remain humble once you do.

12) Keep track of your progress.

While life is short, there are many things that we learn each and every day that helps us grow and reach the next level. But we never seem to notice it due to failing to track our progress.

Always keep a diary and write down everything you experience on a day-to-day basis; it will help you develop an even bigger appreciation of yourself moving forward, knowing that you managed to outgrow yourself, which is an achievement in itself.

CHAPTER FOURTEEN

DONATE MONEY

Success is something that you have to define for yourself, and no one can do it for you. Success could mean a sense of giving back to the world and making a difference. It could mean a sense of accomplishment and career progression.

It could mean being able to do the things you love. It could mean being able to provide the best possible upbringing for your children.

If you want real happiness within you then help the needy one without any expectations it will provide you real joy and calmness's

We did a lot of studies and hard work then earn money for whom. if you think this we will come to know money is only the way that can full feel the basic needs of our life. You should earn money and always be a milliner so you can help others.

If we do good then all other person will do good, never think it will come to you. Defiantly it will come back with us with great joy and happiness.

If you read the happy rich man biography then you come to know that they used to do denotation.

In every religion is saying about to help each other's in all aspects. One day we have to leave this earth without taking any think so I think in the last we have to return back to the needy one.

Giving money to those in need can be a personally satisfying experience, but there is a choice between donating nationally and internationally through charities or giving directly to those around you. This essay will consider the merits of both approaches.

The first advantage of providing direct support is that you can know exactly how your money is being spent. For example, if you give money directly to people in your local village or town, you can see where it has gone. When you donate to larger charitable organisations, on the other hand, you are not sure how much will actually be given to those in need as opposed going on other costs such as administration and expensive marketing campaigns. Another benefit is that you can see the impacts on those you are helping, which can lead not only to great personal satisfaction but also to respect from others in the local community who appreciate the work you do.

There are advantages, however, in giving to charities that are national and international. First and foremost there is the choice of good causes. Locally the kinds of places to help may be limited, but in larger organisations you can get involved in such activities as sponsoring a child or conserving wildlife. Not only this, donating to larger charities with an international reach means having the knowledge that you are involved in issues of fundamental global importance, such as curing diseases and human rights, or helping those caught up in tragic environmental events, such as flooding, earthquakes and famines.

given the benefits of both, I would argue that an individual should make their own choice based on their personal preferences and whichever provides them with the most personal satisfaction. What is crucial is that we continue to give to those who are more in need than ourselves.

I am now sharing the examples of some donator they doing good for society.

Hannah Taylor – The Ladybug Foundation: When she was 5-years-old, Hannah Taylor saw a homeless man eating out of a garbage can on a cold winter day. For the next year she constantly asked her parents: "Why? Why couldn't everyone just share what they have to end homelessness?". At age 8, Hannah founded The Ladybug Foundation which has raised over 3 million dollars to fight homelessness in Canada. Hannah is also the founder of a second, separate charity, The Ladybug Foundation Education Program Inc., through which she created "makeChange: The Ladybug Foundation Education Program", a K-12 resource for use in schools across Canada to empower young people to get involved and "makeChange" in their worlds.

Craig Kielburger – We.org: One morning over breakfast, 12-year-old Craig Kielburger was flipping through the newspaper when he stopped short on a story: Iqbal Masih, a 12-year-old former child slave in Pakistan, had been murdered because he spoke up for human rights. In that moment, Craig realized he could have been Iqbal but for the fate of where he had been born. From there, Craig determined he had to do something and with the help of some classmates and his brother, WE (then Free The Children) was born – an organization that empowers with a mission to free children and their families to lift themselves from poverty and exploitation. The team has also created WE Villages Adopt a Village, dedicated to development that provides access to five key pillars—education, clean water and sanitation, health care, food security, and alternative income— a combination of key interventions that empower a community to help lift themselves out of poverty.

Jonas Corona – Love in the Mirror: When Jonas Corona was 6 he and his Mom would make monthly visits to the local homeless shelter to volunteer. The experience of seeing not only adults but also kids in need inspired Jonas to begin his own organization. Jonas says "every kid should look in the mirror and love themselves" and thus came the name "Love in the Mirror". The mission of Love in the Mirror is to inspire young people to make a difference through their volunteer commitment of providing disadvantaged youth and their families with basic necessities.

Jamsetji Tata

• Lifetime Donations: $102.4 Billion

Jamsetji Tata is the world's biggest philanthropist of the last century with donations worth $102.4 billion, much ahead of Bill Gates, Warren Buffett and more. He was also ranked first in the "Hurun Philanthropists of the Century" (2021).

Although he is no more in this world, his philanthropic contributions are making an admirable change in society.

Serena Williams

• Lifetime Donations: $1 Million

Famously known as the leading tennis player, Serena Williams founded The Serena Williams Foundation, which donates to education, social welfare and community development. She is also the woman behind "Yetunde Price Nursing Scholarship" which was established in association with the California Community Foundation.

Other charities that Serena supports include Common Ground Foundation, Elton John AIDS Foundation, Build African Schools, Great Ormond Street Hospital, Driving Force Giving Circle, Hearts of Gold, and World Education.

J.K. Rowling

• Lifetime Donations: $160 Million

J.K. Rowling is not just famous for her Harry Potter book series but is
Oprah Winfrey
• Lifetime Donations: $240 Million

An American Talk Show host, actress, and author, Oprah Winfrey makes to the list of Top Charitable People in the world due to her donations of millions of dollars to fund charities and different interests.

Her foundation, The Oprah Winfrey Foundation work towards supporting the inspiration, empowerment, and education of women, children, and families around the globe. She once said, "Think about what you have to give, not in terms of dollars because I believe that your life is about service. It's about what you came to give the world, to your children, to your family."

also recognized for her exemplary work in philanthropy.

Her international nonprofit organisation, Lumos aids orphaned children in troubled situations in finding their families or providing them with a home to live in. She also showed her support for the Charity Comic Relief. She donated more than £17 million for Comic Relief. that she raised from the sale of 'Quidditch Through the Ages' and 'Fantastic Beasts and Where to Find Them.'

Mark Zuckerberg & Priscilla Chan

• Lifetime Donations: $2.7 Billion

An American media magnate, billionaire, and famous philanthropist, Mark Zuckerberg along with his wife Priscilla Chan donated around $25 million in the struggle against Ebola. They have also donated $75 million to San Francisco General Hospital through the Silicon Valley Community Foundation.

They both once said, "We will spend our lives working to make sure future generations have the greatest opportunities possible."

Azim Hashim Premji

• Lifetime Donations: $21 Billion

Another name on the list of top 10 charitable people is Azim Premji, the very famous Indian businessman and Chairman of Wipro Limited. Azim Premji Foundation works for the betterment of disadvantaged and marginalised sections of society by offering them immediate care, access to essential services, and the possibility of a dignified future.

He once said that he strongly believes that those of us, who are privileged to have wealth, should contribute significantly to try and create a better world for the millions who are far less privileged than us.

Bill Gates & Melinda Gates

• Lifetime Donations: $28 Billion

The Cofounder and Chairman of the World's big tech giant Microsoft, Bill Gates along with one of the most powerful women and his ex-wife Melinda Gates is involved in a lot of philanthropic work.

Through the Bill and Melinda Gates Foundation, both of them are trying to fight poverty, disease, and inequity around the world. In a recent move in July 2022, Bill Gates poured another $20bn into the charitable foundation.

Warren Buffett

• Lifetime Donations: $48 Billion

The legendary investor & Chairman and CEO of Berkshire Hathaway, Warren Buffett has pledged for years to give away the bulk of his fortune to the Bill & Melinda Gates Foundation.

While serving as the Trustee (2006-2021) of the Foundation, he helped shape the vision and develop strategies to address some of the world's most challenging inequities.

CHAPTER FIFTEEN

Join a Politics Party

Be The Part of country Politics for the well-being of our society.

Where a person is wealthy enough to be completely independent and sees a situation in society that he (she) feels could be improved by genuine personal advocacy, then they should step forward and speak on behalf of those disadvantaged. This, sadly, is at odds with many politicians' motives today, and the con men who win election are frequently the fortune seekers who love attention. The older "grey men" of politics may not have been as charismatic as the TV news stars of today but they were certainly more serious about representing their constituents. The wisdom that they displayed and dispensed is missing in our present system.

Peoples should join politics ..

• People should join politics so that they can become proactive in their welfare,

• People can become responsible in attending mandatory attendance for civic job planning, design and bill auditing.

• People should become active in politics to join panels where discussions are held for budgeting and planning of resources, money and utility of their wards and panchayats,

• People should join politics so that this nationalism snake is stumped on its head and development of wards and panchayats as mentioned in our Constitution has to be done on urgent basis.

• People should join politics as the last resort to help country save itself from its antidemocratic groups operating.

• People should join politics to establish constitution and uphold its fundamental rights.

• People should join politics to keep Country a republic and not become a training ground for religious fundamentalism

Participation in politics and having a deep knowledge or interest is a matter of choice, much like having interest in music or sports.

However, unlike some of the other activities, politics has an impact on all spheres of life, like our job regulations, the infrastructure development of our nation, public services rendered, law and order, education environment, and even whether we can marry our loved man or woman. Hence, one must at least be aware of what is happening in the political world, and which leader or party stands for what policies. With growing polarisation in many countries, knowledge of politics may help us avoid many pitfalls.

This helps us in making wise choices for the betterment of our own lives, and the nation we live in.

First reason to be a politician is that politics is an arena where most pivotal decisions are made. If we pause and think about it, some of the most important decisions in the history of our country and world are taken by politicians. Five-year plans and centralized economic activity, emergency, economic liberalization, Right to information and Right to education, demonetization- all these decisions were taken by politicians and changed India forever- for better or worse. Big reforms happen through both social movements and political will. However, we know that in India, it is the elected representatives where the buck stops. So let's occupy these positions and create both incremental and transformational change.

Second reason for being a politician is the scope of work and the sheer scale at which politicians can make an impact is unimaginable. The resources that our representatives have are incomparable to any CSR budget. For FY 2018-19, the total CSR budget as reported to the Ministry of Corporate Affairs was 11,867 Crore while the total Union Budget was 24,00,000 Crore. Our elected representatives decide where this money is allocated. Just imagine the impact right allocation and efficient delivery of these funds can have on the lives of 1.2 billion people, if there is political will and right leadership.

Third and probably the most important reason is that we must represent the voice of the people, using the opportunities our country has given us. President Mukherjee once said,"We should have 1,000 members of parliament." He remarked that it is difficult to truly represent the country as diverse and as populated as India, through a few hundred MPs. And do the voices in the parliament represent India? 50% population in India is below the age of 30, but only 6% MPs are less than the age of 35 years and most of them are from political families.

50% population in India is women, but only 14.39% members in Lok Sabha are women. While we can't change the number of MPs allowed by tomorrow, we can enter local politics today. We can harness the power of the local panchayats and municipal councils, get elected in these areas and try to represent and serve the people of India.

Let's occupy politics. why can't we be the creators of impact which can truly touch lives of people through the most powerful vehicle of public service- politics.

We at Indian School of Democracy hope to support many of you in this journey. We conduct short term and long-term programs to nurture principled leaders with moral courage and imagination, to enter politics. It is time we rethink public leadership and politics. India needs new leaders in our parliaments, assemblies, panchayats and municipal corporations -- leaders who are true representatives of the society. We need representatives and not rulers and we think our generation has the power, potential and duty to serve through politics.

Government and Politics is a fantastic A Level that has shown us just how great an influence Politics has on us and has broken the illusion that we are disconnected from it.

Recent months have seen the Scottish Independence referendum, attacks on free speech in Paris and, crucially, the General Election in May is now on the horizon.

Aside from the huge benefits that this course brings with it in terms of an understanding of events that are happening around us, here are our

Top 5 Reasons to join Politics:

1. Politics Helps You to Know Your Rights

The course has allowed us to see beyond our initial belief that we have no real say in the running of our country. It has truly educated us on a fundamental part of our society and has helped us to understand that if we engage in political processes, using the pressure points built into the system, then every individual really does have the opportunity to change the world.

2. Politics Clarifies What You Yourself Believe

Studying the things we have studied has given us the opportunity to discover our own political beliefs and to see in much greater detail the benefits and disadvantages of the vast array of political ideologies that are present in the world today. Being able to express what you believe accurately and concisely is extremely useful, and forces you to really look at yourself!

3. Politics is a Living, Breathing Subject

In Politics, textbooks go out of date the day they are published. Why? Because the political landscape changes every day, with new examples appearing constantly in the media. Picking which examples to use in your answers to essay questions is really exciting as something that has happened on the day you are taking your A Level exams can appear in your response!

4. Politics Helps You to Understand Our Nation's Parties

After just one term of the subject we have learnt about democracy and our rights, ideologies and party policies, the Constitution and Parliament. With the knowledge gained from the classroom, we have been able to watch events unfold worldwide, have seen our leaders' reactions to these events and have come to understand these reactions as demonstrations of what we have learned.

5. Politics Prepares You for Adult Life

The world of British politics really opens up to teenagers after our eighteenth birthdays, with the vote giving us the ability to change our nation and allow the principles we hold dear to thrive. With this in mind, it could easily be said that Government and Politics is the most applicable subject on offer at any school, and is a subject that people should be encouraged to take due to nothing less than the way it prepares you for entering the adult world.

Political parties play a vital role in a democracy. A country can only be considered democratic if its elections are proven to constitute a real competition between two or among several candidates who may be backed by political parties or are running independently.

Political parties are organized groups of people who share a set of similar political aims and opinions and aim to influence public policy by getting their candidates elected. The main functions of these parties are to present their candidates and electoral campaigns to the electorate. But they also perform many other tasks in a democratic country. For one, they serve as institutionalized mediators between society and the duly elected representatives who are responsible for deciding and implementing policies. To illustrate, legislators who are affiliated with a political party and meet with civil society representatives seek opinions from individuals or organizations in the process of formulating public policy. By doing so, they are allowing the demands of their members and supporters to be represented in a parliament and in the government.

In a democratic society, political parties perform key duties, including the following:

• Seeking public policy priorities and civic needs and issues identified by their members and supporters.

• Educating the people how the political and electoral system and general political values work.

• Balancing contrasting demands and turning them into general policies.

• Encouraging citizens to participate in political decisions and turning their opinions into policy options for all.

• Acting as a mediator between the public and the government.

• Choosing and training candidates who are worthy to be elected to public office.

Every political party has internal functions that are determined by external forces, such as political culture, electoral system and legal regulations. But internal processes such as the ideological foundations, party history, personality of leaders and staff members and internal political culture are more influential to a party's internal functions.

In the United States, there is what they call the two-party system. This means that there are two major parties that dominate the elections and the government. Although this nature of political system has its benefits in promoting good for all people, there are those who criticized it for its disadvantages.

To be able to determine whether having two political parties is actually beneficial to a country or not, it is important to know the advantages and disadvantages of having them.

List of Advantages of Political Parties

1. Political parties are able to present political information to the voting population in a manner that is readily understandable.

By doing so, there is order in the country through the representation of broad political philosophy of the group. As a result, voters become aware of every party's stance on certain issues. A good example would be the 2012 Presidential Election between Republican Mitt Romney and Democrat Barack Obama. Each candidate represented major issues of their respective parties to the public.

2. Political parties provide balance through the accommodation of various interests and opinions.

Both political parties are organized groups with differing political views, which make it important for political parties to make decisions that will favor not only few but also all interests and opinions to keep the loyalty of their supporters.

3. Political parties prevent unexpected shifts in political trends that threaten stability in the government.

The US' two-party system helps promote stability in the government because there will only be two parties sharing power, which can dissolve or change coalitions immediately. Now, if voters disagree on one political issue, they would generally understand that the candidates represent bigger issues that need more attention. This discourages voters from giving up their support for their party. Additionally, elected officials will have time to focus on long-term policies that benefit the public.

4. Political parties encourage political participation.

As a democratic nation, America allows its citizens to freely express their opinions and to support the political party that shares their interest and opinion. Unlike China, the US government encourages the public to participate and cast their votes at the polls. Hence, the public can contribute in making significant changes that will benefit everyone.

THE END

9 798888 909340